About Ralph Buckingham's Journey

In 1849, Ralph Buckingham, a younger son of a youngest son of New England Pilgrim stock, went to California from his small-town Connecticut home. Landless, with no inheritance or trade of his own, Ralph sailed around the Horn, then traveled overland from San Francisco to gold country in the Trinity Mountains. He spent four years in northern California, struggling daily to earn enough to build a future.

Sixty years later, back home in Connecticut, Ralph writes his story at the behest of the *Newtown Bee* newspaper man. Well-schooled in spite of his relative poverty, Ralph Buckingham quotes Boswell, Shakespeare, Dickens, Byron, and Sir Walter Scott as he describes the agonies and antics of men sluicing for gold amidst rattlesnakes and mosquitoes where Western civilization had not yet asserted itself. Recounting his adventures and the colorful—and later, famous—characters he met, Ralph describes in lively detail the geography and natural history of the lands where he traveled and worked.

The newspaper columns from 1910—originally titled *Memories of a Forty-Niner*—were preserved by family members for a century, handed down through generations. These *Newtown Bee* articles, now transcribed and edited, tell the story of a young man who went into the wilds with a sharp eye and a sharp mind, and returned to tell those who stayed safely at home how it was to dig for gold when the West was still untamed.

Journey into Gold Country

Memories of a Forty-Niner

℘

Ralph Buckingham

℘

First told in the *Newtown Bee*, 1912–1913

℘

Foreword
by Charles Barker

Jugum Press

Copyright © 2013 by Charles M. Barker
All rights reserved.
First print edition: August 2013

ISBN 978-1-939423-10-8

Editing, footnotes, and design:
Annie Pearson, Jugum Press

Cover by Lisa Tilton Design
Published by Jugum Press
For other ebook formats, see:
www.jugumpress.com

Grateful Acknowledgment: The original edition of the articles by Ralph Buckingham first appeared in his hometown newspaper, the *Newtown Bee*, 1912–1913. The *Newtown Bee* has reported news for the Newtown, Connecticut area since 1877. www.newtownbee.com/

Credits:
1. *Samoset* Passenger List, from "Movements for California from New York" — *Samoset* Passenger List," *New York Herald*, March 24, 1849. From *California Bound* on SFgenealogy:
www.sfgenealogy.com/californiabound/cb085.htm
2. Ralph Buckingham daguerreotype, copy derived from article in *Newtown Bee*, 1912.
3. Photo, Ralph Buckingham headstone, Merritt Barker Hicks.

Original material in 2013 edition of *Journey Into Gold Country: Memories of a Forty-Niner* copyright by Charles M. Barker. All rights reserved.

Contents

Foreword v
I: Going to California 1
    1. Starting Out 1
    2. Brazil 7
    3. Cape Horn 10
    4. Valparaiso 14
    5. Coming to San Francisco 18
II: Into California Gold Country 25
    6. Up the Sacramento to the Stanislaus 25
    7. The Mining Camp on Carson's Creek 29
    8. Ben, Phillips, and the Working Company 34
    9. Vigilance Committee Times 40
III: Into the Trinities 47
    10. Traveling to the Trinity River 47
    11. Pests 52
    12. Placer Mining in the Trinities 57
    13. Life in Trinity County 64
    14. Dennis B. Mooney and the Stockton Road 67
    15. The Disputed Claim 70
IV: Heading Back 77
    16. Starting for Home 77
    17. Leaving California 83
    18. Sailing Home 87
V: Back Home 93
    19. Home in Connecticut – 1853 93
Appendix 99
    A. The Buckingham Family 99
    B. Newtown Bee Entries 101
    C. Editor's Notes 103
Index 104

Foreword

RALPH BUCKINGHAM'S MEMOIR came to me from my grandmother, Juliette Beach Barker, by way of her commitment to primogeniture, the succession of property, wealth, or influence considered to be the right of the oldest male heir in a family. After the death of her only brother, she took it upon herself to further the family legacy by giving me this unusual tale, along with her Daughters of the American Revolution membership file, which documents the Beach/Buckingham ancestry back to 1712. The source material came as a set of hand-set newspaper columns written by Ralph for the *Newtown Bee*.

Ironically, the voyage Ralph set upon to the California Gold Rush was prompted by being a casualty of primogeniture, since he was the fifth of his parents' six sons.

New Milford was founded in 1707, a mill town on the banks of the Housatonic River in the foothills of the Berkshire Mountains, eighty miles north of New York City. Lumber and paper mills abounded along the river, and Ralph spent his youth "sawing," according to my grandmother.

The landed gentry of New England that arrived before the Revolution were generally status-conscious English folks, who soon put later Western European immigrants to work at their enterprises, building their hegemony. Family status was an unseen but guiding hand as late as the first half of the twentieth century, as I remember scowls and comments of disapproval of the childhood friends I chose and the oft-delivered directive from my father, when visiting others' homes, to "Tell them who you are!"

If this Forty-niner's narrative seems garrulous, remember Ralph's age at the time of writing: eighty-five. He was well read and ahead of his time in many ideas, though his prejudices on race were those of a pre-Civil War Democrat. He was the first in the area in methods and equipment in the home and on the farm. He had a marble-lined pig sty because, he said, pigs were clean animals. A journal at age twenty speaks each day of sawing at the lumber yard and then at night reading or discussing science, religion, and philosophy with a friend.

Ralph and I share some confusion over who exactly we are, but this tale reveals Ralph's character embedded in the social context of the time. Our voyages West in search of ourselves were 130 years apart, but were motivated by a similar distaste for the limits of choice that family allegiance required.

Charles M. Barker
July 2013

I: Going to California

1. Starting Out

I HAVE A PLEASANT PERSONAL acquaintance with the *Newtown Bee* man, as he is familiarly known among us. As I am inclined to speak of my experiences to the point of ridiculousness, I didn't think as *The Bee* man does that it would be entertaining to write for the paper as he urges me to do. But I submit this and what follows to his discretion.

I have good ancestry, as proved by *The Buckingham Family*[1], compiled under the auspices of William A. Buckingham, the war governor of Connecticut, and the near ancestry of great grandfather Nathaniel of Milford, one of the original proprietors of New Milford, who established his sixth and youngest son Abel there, whose sixth and youngest son was my father Gilbert, I being the fifth of his six sons.

My father and mother had five children each by previous marriage: my father, four sons and one daughter; my mother, three sons and two daughters. On their marriage, with me being the eldest of two sons and one daughter, they had thirteen in all. My father and mother were the wisest persons I ever knew. The twigs were bent but not broken. Our wildcat tempers were unrestrained, except when they interfered with the commonwealth. We were purred over, licked, bit, and scratched, as the case demanded. The experience of the teeth and claws of others taught us the proper use of our own. We were not an unhappy family, fed and clothed on the direct product of the farm, and educated so as not to be conspicuous for our ignorance. I had five brothers and three sisters who were school teachers. We were not considered lacking in character. My father was a large man, six feet, broad-shouldered, of some cultivation. We were all smaller.

---

[1] *The Buckingham Family: Or The Descendants Of Thomas Buckingham, One Of The First Settlers Of Milford Connecticut (1872)*, Frederick William Chapman, Editor
www.archive.org/stream/buckinghamfamily00chap/buckinghamfamily00chap_djvu.txt

I inherited a good constitution, nothing more than ordinary intellect, but the temper of a wildcat, which did not always go before my judgment, but was recognized in my intercourse in savage and civilized life among all sorts and conditions of men.

I am now 85 years old. When I look at a daguerreotype taken in '49 in Sacramento City, before I went to the barber's and put on a boiled shirt, and when my grandchildren say, "Why, Grandpa, was that ever you?" I don't know. I think I knew him when I was young.

Ralph Buckingham, Sacramento, 1853

Boarding the *Samoset* in New York

I WAS 21 YEARS OLD THEN. I went to New York to get passage to California, having barely capital for an outfit, having been descended through many generations of the younger sons of large families. I was alone on my first visit to the city. I found the ship *Samoset*[2] waiting for passengers and freight. It looked well to my unaccustomed eyes.

I had heard much of sea life and had the usual boyish desire for the sea. In Richard Henry Dana's *Two Years Before the Mast*, which has become a classic on sea life, he speaks of the choice of a mate to fill a vacancy, and the captain tried to choose Tim Hall from Maine. One of the passengers on the *Samoset* was Captain [James] Dennis Hall with his young wife; the deck load was his: the hull of an iron steamboat to run on the San Joaquin and Sacramento River, where the steamer *Minot* was blown up by explosion of her boilers a few years afterwards.

---

[2] "Movements for California from New York— *Samoset* Passenger List," *New York Herald*, March 24, 1849. From *California Bound* on SFgenealogy: http://www.sfgenealogy.com/californiabound/cb085.htm

I: Going to California

I thought if he was a passenger with so much at stake, the ship must be good. The carrying of the steamboat as a deck load was perilous, as was proved when the most perilous incident of the voyage was encountered between Rio de Janeiro and Cape Horn, a tempest that partly broke the lashings and would have carried away the masts.

Our ship was loaded to the limit with freight and passengers. The discomfort can best be described as Dr. Thompson said: "The only advantage of sea life over a state prison is the pleasant prospect of being drowned."[3]

> New York Herald
> March 24, 1849
>
> ### Movements for California
> ### from New York
>
> We published, yesterday, a list of a few passengers by the splendid ship *Samoset*, Captain Hollis, which sailed on Thursday, for San Francisco. We now give a full and complete list:--
>
> ...
>
> **Additional passengers:**
> Alverson, A.B., Baltimore
> Anderson, William
> Arnold, Austin, Delaware
> Arthur, J.D.
>
> ...
>
> Bonner, D.D., Baltimore
>
> ...
>
> Buckingham, Robert, Delaware
>
> ...
>
> Hall, Captain James, and lady, Boston
>
> ...
>
> "A gentleman who was accompanying his friends down the bay, became so much excited that he paid his passage and remained on board."

Samoset Passenger List, including Ralph Buckingham (misidentified)

---

[3] From Boswell's Life of Samuel Johnson.

"The Seasickness!"

IT HAS BEEN SAID OFTEN, "You go abroad, you are afraid you will die during sickness." Seasickness is not universally confined to the greenhorn; old sailors have it after a stay ashore. Some never have it. I had it to the limit. It was about a month before my stomach would retain food.

It was cold weather on the twenty-second of March when we left New York and beat our way through the chop sea of the Gulf Stream, steering for the coast of Africa to take advantage of the trade winds, until we sighted the Cape Verde Islands, crossed the equator, and took the southeast trades and steered for Rio de Janeiro.

Most of the passengers were from the state of New York, some from the south and west as far as Michigan. I was an obscure unit among some two hundred sick and miserable; none I had ever seen before. I endeavored to make myself as inconspicuous as possible. A man from the south said to me, "I know a fellow where you came from. He looks and acts like you. He is quite a chap; don't say much."

Discomfort and Friendship

WE WERE AT THE limit of endurance of discomfort and some inclined to be quarrelsome. A fight was of daily occurrence, when Captain Hollis, a giant in physique, would enter the scene, throwing the crowd aside on both hands as if they were so many puppies, and taking the fighters, one in each hand at arm's length, saying, "No fighting here," and order was restored.

The growling was constant. The food coarse, prepared by Negro cooks, and necessarily in short supply for a prospective long voyage with so many to feed. I answered the growlers once by saying, "It is as good as I expected." You must be a damned fool, to start on such a voyage as this and expect such a life. Who is the greatest damned fool: you, in expecting a bill of fare like a New York eating house to choose from, or me, expecting what I get?

I was a boy, the eleventh of thirteen children, well brought up by wise parents to paddle my own canoe, fight my own battles, and take the consequences of my wildcat temper which, with my ordinary physical and mental temperament, has proved the most valuable of any possession. Few men know themselves; only by experience comes knowledge. I was soon to become acquainted with myself and make the acquaintance of others.

The between deck was clear from stem to stern, our bunks in tiers on the sides, three in height, with a table through the center where we ate, and our sea chests on each side for seats. We were packed at the table as close as we could sit, each man on his own chest. I took my seat, but vacated it when seasick. If a man had a peculiarity, he had a nickname. Mine, I found, was "the quiet fellow." Jake Arthur of Kinderhook, New York, was great on ridiculing and nicknames. My neighbor at the table was a red-headed, red-bearded man. He was called "Molasses Candy." As I returned from being seasick, I went back to my seat. He said, "You are on my seat."

I spoke quietly. "This is my seat. I took it on as my chest when I came abroad. I have been sick, but it is mine and I shall keep it."

"You will get out of it, or you will be put out."

I damned and cursed him to the limit of language, amid the cheers and yells of the delighted and astonished passengers. (He was not popular.) I heard them say, "I never heard that fellow swear before. I did not think it was in him."

My astonishment was equal to theirs that he did not wipe the deck with me. He did not come in. I had plenty of friends immediately. I was a safe man to tie to. I would neither do nor suffer injustice. My audacity had conquered. I was never again molested. They knew and I knew that I would fight like a wild cat to the last, and I found what an asset a temper is when needed. I had friends after my own heart, glorious good fellows, who would neither do nor suffer wrong. We had some fun of a rough kind.

There were two classes of passengers. A few lived with the captain (like Captain Hall and his wife), and several others were in a deck house. The most of us were between decks, as I have said, in an open room. There we were allowed freedom consistent with the safety and working of the ship. All sorts, polished and in the rough, including an Irishman who had escaped after a failed plot against the government with a price on his head. Some men were of the manner and interests of gentlemen. A quiet gentleman was known as a well-descended and well-bred man.

Crossing the Line

WE WERE USED TO HIJINKS aboard. The crossing of the line[4], as described in Marryatt's[5] records, was initiated with variations. It was near midnight, an ideal night: clear, with just enough wind for seaway so that liberty could be allowed. When the crossing was proclaimed by the captain, stores of eatables and drinkables were brought out. If one was found in his bunk, the half-naked savages would drench him with a bucket of seawater. Speeches and all sorts of songs with all sorts of choruses were the order. We had some like Dickens. They dropped into poetry and anything of note was found the next day on the post board in rhyme, more or less doggerel.

A prominent character was D.D. Bonner, who had been editor of a paper, was one of the original Washington families. He had become dissipated and then been a temperance lecturer; a big, stalwart fellow, ready with head and hand. In the early morning in their drowsy state, the passengers aboard heard all the noises of the farmyard: the cocks crowing, hens cackling, turkeys gobbling, pigs squealing, bulls bellowing, horses neighing, so exact in imitation we would fancy them real. Bonner could sing a good song and, at the end could cup, the exact imitation of a frog diving into the water. Towards the end of the voyage, Bonner described in rhyme the incidents of the voyage, which he sent home to be published and sent to the friends of anyone upon their subscription to his paper. My friends were amused by it.

Bonner lectured on temperance aboard ship, but alas, at Rio de Janeiro, he relapsed; the reaction from sea-going misery was too much. Bonner got on a spree. The police were soldiers with guns and bayonets, and they attempted to arrest him. He put down five of them and then escaped to the ship and the protection of the American flag on the deck of the ship *Samoset*.

---

[4] A maritime ceremony celebrating a sailor's first crossing of the Equator.

[5] Captain Frederick Marryat (1792-1848) was an English Navy officer and inventor of a widely used system for maritime flag signaling, "Marryat's Code." He was also a popular novelist, whose works were models for both C.S. Forester and Patrick O'Brian.

I: Going to California

2. Brazil

Rio de Janeiro

ON CROSSING THE EQUATOR we stood for the southwest, the southeast trade winds for Cape Frio and Rio de Janeiro. At sunset one day we saw some protuberances between us and the setting sun above the water. These were the mountaintops of distant land. Our course was diagonal towards it.

Next morning the land was on our right through the day as we approached the mouth of the harbor, which we gained at sunset. One of the grandest sights I ever saw: at the left of the entrance the mountains were higher than on the right, forming one of the singular panoramas of nature. It is called Lord Hood on the chart. The outline on the skyline is of a giant at rest, the mountains forming the features and body with arms folded over the breast and the feet at the left entrance of the harbor. A cone called the Sugar Loaf, so steep as to be inaccessible, is some 1,100 feet high. There is a story of an American sailor climbing the peak and leaving the flag of our country floating from the summit, where it wore out, none being able to remove it.

On the north side stands the castle of San Antonio, where all entering the harbor must report. The sunset guns had been fired at the approach and, like music softened by distance, the speaking trumpet hail came over the water:

"Americana ship a-h-o-y!"

The captain answered with speaking trumpet. "Hello."

"What ship is that? Where are you from and where are you bound?"

"Ship *Samoset*, from New York, bound for California."

"Good-night!"

This was immediately shouted to the distant fort, which passed it on to the city ten miles away. The wind died away and we anchored a short distance within.

In the morning, the panorama in which we were surrounded is said to be the grandest and most beautiful on earth. Cone-like mountains covered with the dense vegetation of the tropics to the summit, the sides and valleys between covered with orange and other fruit groves and coffee plantations, with white residences of the inhabitants and old churches and monastic buildings. The forts on the islands and the points and the city at the head of the harbor with the white houses and red tile roofs, the palm trees and tropic vegetation was all of beauty and grandeur a fertile imagination could form and that we could realize.

Everyone on board got out his best togs to go ashore, but we were in the land of "manna" (to-morrow.) We supposed a harbor master would immediately board us. No communication must be had with our boat until he had. None came. So we lay in the heated sunshine, cursing the Spanish proverb, "Never do today what can be put off until tomorrow, for perhaps tomorrow it will not want to be done." No breeze to carry us forward, so we got out a kedge anchor, carried it forward, let go, and the passengers warped it up again and again. Thus we came up.

At sunset, at length, a canopied boat of the revenue officers came along side, followed by a fleet of boats surrounding the ship. And when the regulations had been complied with, the American consul delivered a lecture on our behavior ashore:

> No weapons, not even a penknife, must be carried.
> Nothing must be brought aboard except by the agency seller.
> Not a basket of fruit as there was an export duty that must be complied with.

There was a ship from Philadelphia, some of whose passengers were in the prison [at Rio de Janeiro]. Their ship sailed without them. The consul, [backed by] the ships of war of the United States, demanded their release. They then came as passengers on our ship, to our discomfort.

Ashore in Rio

MANY WENT ASHORE THAT night. I with my friends waited until morning. The confinement, monotony, and misery was atoned for by the most enjoyable day of my life. First, of course, we went for a breakfast, to our content. Then, with the accumulated energy of fifty days, swung out for a tramp of sightseeing among foreign sights and scenes among foreign people.

The city was laid out in squares like a chess-board: a vacant square surrounded by built up squares; the vacant square with a stone fountain in the center, which was supplied with ample water from an aqueduct we followed for miles in the surrounding mountains. The fountains were the water supply of the city; no piping to the dwellings. The woman-slaves carried a keg with a ring pad on their heads, with unerring poise untouched by hand—the most graceful walkers imaginable. They sailed with footsteps invisible.

There were practically no beasts of burden, few wheeled vehicles, and no wharves for the loading or unloading of ships. The slaves carried everything on their heads with the ring pads—sometimes several under a heavy article, brought as near shore as possible in large boats. The Negroes in procession were unloading a large cargo of U.S. flour, with a barrel on each head on end from the boats to the warehouse across the square.

There is no more instructive place in the city than the market to see the productions and how they are used. This is enclosed in a wall some twenty feet high, occupying a square, with the gate at each side, the streets meeting in the center with a stone fountain, everything clean and orderly, the soldiers as policemen with gun and bayonet, the Negroes in multitude, all shades of inhabitants "from snow-white, dark to sooty," the dark prevailing. From those recently landed from East Africa to those who had been there for several generations. Well fed and clothed, with the minimum suited to conditions. There appeared to be no color line socially, though I saw no officials but the white men. This was under the Empire, the Braganza Portuguese dynasty.

We rambled among the hills and hillside grounds, behaved like gentlemen, and were treated as such. We would come to the proprietor's gate and ask permission to enter his premises. With the most dignified politeness, the sign was "Enter" his orange groves and coffee plantations. It was a revelation to pick ripe oranges from the trees, to us who had never tasted any but green ones ripened afterwards. We visited churches during the Roman Catholic services, the same in all languages, and were impressed with the word Catholic. It was a festal day.

Brazil is not a food-producing country at present. There was at that time much trade of American flour. This has become the cereal product of Argentina, whose coffee and rubber products can supply the world.

A sight and sound ever remembered was the close of the day officially, the discharge of the great guns from the castle of San Antonio at the entrance of the harbor ten miles away. The guns were in view on the summit, and the discharge was seen long before the report was heard. When it came, it was echoed from mountain to mountain in continuation, seemingly endless.

The peril of the sea depends on the efficiency of the sailors to discipline and command. Much has been written of the "jolly sailor" in contrast to the hard sea life, and in the shore reaction he seems so. But when at sea, by necessity he must obey orders at peril of life, and he is a chronic growler. Many of them are life failures. Some had been mates, and it was said one had been captain of a vessel. Hardened and reckless, they came aboard drunk and disorderly. They were terrors. One was covered with the scars of many battles would fight with all, particularly the first mate. The captain, the only one aboard who was capable of handling him, came between.

"You will not whip my mate or anyone else. Go below." The captain said, "I shall have to half kill him to bring him to his duty."

The sailor reeling, staggering, fell overboard. We had just left the harbor, and the lee shore was dangerous and the ship could not be hove to. As he struck the water, he was sober in an instant, swimming for his life. A rope was thrown. He caught it, took a turn around his body, and then was drawn through the water swiftly and hauled aboard. He vanished in the forecastle; the next day on duty, he was the efficient sailor as usual.

The land soon went down in the distance, and the wintry voyage around Cape Horn was before us.

3. Cape Horn

As we left Rio de Janeiro, we came into the stormiest latitude of the world, the "Roaring Forties." The comprehension of facts and the action accordingly is the science of the sailor. I had become somewhat familiar with the sea-terms and knew most of the ropes. I could box the compass, and when an order was given, I knew what it meant.

The heat of the sun in the tropics causes expansion of air and water, and a rise and flow towards the poles, with a consequent flow of the cold air and water to take its place. The centrifugal action of the revolution of the earth makes the western shores of the continent a higher temperature than the eastern. Thus, the United States and Canada are practically in a higher latitude than Europe, the stormy Atlantic being more affected by winds blowing over vast stretches of

I: Going to California

land, and more affected than the Pacific by storms, especially outside the tropics where cold air meets the warm. The voyage between the United States and Europe is more subject to storms than any on earth. The voyage from Rio de Janeiro to Cape Horn is subject to the same or worse conditions, and the storms off the coasts of Argentina and Patagonia are to be reckoned with.

It is seldom I have seen a sea picture true to fact. The wind blows steadily, usually, and in proportion to length of time, in one direction is the rise of the waves uniform in height. So looking across the water, the water on the horizon is the same in a storm as in a calm. A man standing on the shore can see the surface about six miles, the rotundity being about one foot to the mile. So the picture of the mountain wave in the distance is not found in fact. The highest wave is some thirty or forty feet. In a stormy time, the ship is kept diagonally to the course of the wave, which are moving although the water does not run. When a heavy wind is encountered, sails are taken in on the mizzen and main masts, and the sail close-reefed on fore-mast, the fore-topsail with jib to bowsprit being in evidence of sufficient height to draw when the hull is down between the waves. Of course, I speak from imperfect knowledge. On general principles, these are facts.

Our ship was good, but had too much deck load. For stability, the load must be below the water, as near the keel as possible. Our captain had never been around Cape Horn, being an East India man, so we were unprepared for what we encountered. The steamboat on saddles were bolted to the deck. Coal bin, deckhouses for cabin passengers and sailors, cooking galleys, pigsties, and so on were all on the working deck. The between decks were occupied by seconds. The fore and main hatches, each about six feet square, were unclosed for benefit of air.

One night the second mate was in charge. The increasing gale made a sea running greater than I had ever seen. I spoke to him as we were looking to windward of the sublimity of the sight.

"Yes," says he, "when you don't know but you will be in hell in five minutes, it is somewhat exciting."

I went below. I had a lower berth. The water had been dashing over and, with the unclosed hatches, had come down and, with the roll of the ship, had wet my bed. I was stowing my bed into an upper berth when a crash came like a thunder bolt and a shock that broke everything loose, some 300 sea chests secured by cleats to the deck, with a large safe amid ship.

The ship was under water.

Two streams six feet square were pouring down and the ship rolling, so that the decks were at an angle of thirty or forty degrees, with the safe and all the chests going from side to side. The safe we expected to see go through the ship's side. There was no doubt in our minds that death was but a few minutes away. The helpless agony was indescribable. The screams and cries of the passengers filled the air. The deck load of coal and pigs came down with the water, the pigs squealing as frightened as any of us.

I gained the deck and went with the dash of water to leeward. The captain was roaring orders above the tempest. The weather bulwarks were carried away level with the deck; the top rail, some twelve inches in diameter, was as broken as a pipe stem. The braces of the yards were gone, but some order was brought out of chaos by the captain and efficient sailors, whom I found were under such discipline and efficiency of the captain, who could hold his poise in "the wreck of matter and the crush of worlds."[6]

As soon as security was made on deck, attention was given below. The safe was secured. There was some two feet of water which, the lower hatches being secure, had not gone into the hold. The captain, with lantern, examined the weather side to see if damage had been done. But the force of the wave had been above, although the sensation was as though the ship had been thrown against a rock.

The captain shouted, "Form a line to the deck. Stand in your tracks, pass the pails back and forth and back, and be quick about it."

We were thankful to receive orders. Some of us who were not helpless from fear sprang into line, and a stream of water the size of the bucket was going to the deck. The ship had been broached; it fell into the trough of the waves and had been struck by one. Sometimes ships

---

[6] Joseph Addison, "Cato," 1713:
  The stars shall fade away, the sun himself
  Grow dim with age, and Nature sink in years;
  But thou shalt flourish in immortal youth,
  Unhurt amid the war of elements,
  The wreck of matter, and the crush of worlds.

go down in such a case. All this had happened in much less time than it is told.

At length, daylight came with no abatement of wind or sea. The ship shifted, rolling fearfully. The hold was opened, and some cargo was thrown overboard. The deck load, more valuable, was stowed below, so we rode on a more even keel. But the sea was such that another such stroke would break loose the steamboat, taking with it the main and fore-masts, with inevitable destruction.

So two days and nights passed in anticipation of death in every wave, with two men at the steering wheel and all hands on deck. But the hull under us was sound, and we weathered the storm. The days were shortening, the dead of winter was upon us, snow and sleet freezing, hatches closed, everything wet and sodden. (I slept on a wet bed for a month.)

The cooking was difficult: the necessaries of life were all we could expect. At length, we sighted Staten Land, an island separated from Tierra del Fuego. The next day we had a favorable wind and a southwesterly course; we sighted Cape Horn, a saddleback island, where we lay in a calm with a smooth-surface sea, but with the mighty swells uninterrupted as they roll around the world.

That night a gale came from the southwest, and we were obliged to beat against it and escape a lee shore. For a week we encountered this prevailing wintry wind. We made a latitude of about sixty. The days were about six hours long. It was a happy time when we turned northward with this southwest wind on our port quarter. In a week we left the snow and sleet, and could dry our clothes and beds.

Nature at Sea

THE MOST REMARKABLE SCENE was the bird-life. Clouds of them followed the ship, from the largest seabird, the albatross, down to the Cape pigeon, the size of the domestic dove. We caught one albatross with a baited hook to examine, its wings from tip to tip measuring eleven and one-half feet, with brown back and white under. All sea birds are inedible. With great spreads of wings in proportion to size of body, they are adapted to perpetual flight, sailing with seldom motion of the wings.

Of fish, we saw the porpoises of the Gulf Stream, the black fish like a miniature whale. The flying fish of the tropics would come out of the water in flocks, flying some quarter of a mile. We would find them on deck in the morning sometimes, where they had struck the sails or rigging in the night. We saw a few whales in the Atlantic Ocean. Some sperm whales, the most valuable in the tropical waters, sometimes broke the monotony.

ଔ

MANY YEARS AFTER, a building connected with a house was burnt. I rode up at full speed, sprung for my horse near the river. Men were running, each with a pail. I shouted, "Form a line to the river. Stand in your tracks, pass the pails back and forth, and be quick about it." I was on the roof and kept the stream going. The heat was such that my face was blistered, but it was effectual. The house was saved. A man shouted, "If we had had a first-rate fire engine here, that house would have been burnt."

4. Valparaiso

WE WERE IN A FAVORABLE wind on our port quarter, hoping to spend the Fourth of July in Valparaiso, but we sighted land on our starboard bow on that day and had a celebration on board. The Stars and Stripes were run up with cheers. The Declaration of Independence was read; the "Star Spangled Banner" was sung with all voices in chorus. Not much feasting.

On the morning of the Fifth we sighted the city, Valparaiso, vale of Paradise. The sight of the city and its immediate environment was not imposing: an unenclosed, open port with barren hills coming to the beach; some places with room for but one street between the bluff and the water. This is the country of earthquakes, and on tramping over these hills we found they were comparatively of recent origin. We found many seashells of the same varieties as on the shore with the living inmates.

But there was no *mañana* here. Before we came to anchor, the harbor master came onboard, an old Swede speaking good English, with a Chileno boatman, followed by a fleet of boats. We were allowed to go ashore with no delay.

I would say a word about the Spanish language. To me it is the easiest, most musical, and softest of any I have ever heard. The names of places and things, when in the alphabet, are known as euphonious. The principal differences are that the "I" is "E," the 'E' is "A," and the "A" is "Aw." Chili is spelt "Chile," pronounced "Chela," the people "Chelanos." Cervantes, the Spanish Shakespeare, wrote *Don Quixote*, which as spelled and pronounced in English would break a Spanish jaw; as spelt in Spanish it's "Quijote," pronounced "Keehota," accented on the second syllable with a long sound. Why these outrages came to be adopted in the English language of the pronouncement of the Latin-derivative languages—Spanish, Italian and French—passes me.

The Chilenos are called the Yankees of South America. We were struck with their seeming vigor. There was a large European population. The harbor master was a Swede who had a Chileno wife. I saw him on a festal day with his daughter on his arm, who I thought the most beautiful girl I ever saw, the clear Scandinavian complexion with roses in the cheeks, the form and carriage, hair, and eyes of Andalusia and Castile.

As usual I went to market to see the productions of the unpromising country, and I was astonished at what I saw. Chile is the California of the south in latitude and productions, but has a much superior climate, not subject to the extremes of drought and flood. Such vegetables and fruits I never saw. There was not a locomotive in South America. The long strings of oxen and the carts from the interior and the capital, Santiago, with trains of pack animals bringing flour and other productions made for a stirring sight. Chile was the granary of the Pacific. All flour from California came there. The lighter boats loading vessels showed great business.

From the deck of our ship looking eastward, especially at sunset, the grandest and most imposing sight was before us. High in the horizon, one hundred miles away but seeming nearer, was the perpetual snow of the Andes: Mount Aconcagua could be seen, with its attendant peaks forming a continuous chain as far north and south in the dim distance. As night came down at sea level, the city lighted up for the night, a higher and mighty world, the highest land on earth except the Himalayas of Asia.

I had for several years in California a partner who had been in Peru and Chile for eleven years. He had been a sailor, but left the ship and established a blacksmith. He had trained native helpers in Valparaiso, where he carried on a successful business doing government work, educated himself in the Spanish language, and could read its literature. He was my most friendly companion. We ate from the same dish and joined blankets[7] when we slept, so I was informed of South American life, its customs and manners up to the time of which I am speaking.

In reading since, I have been much impressed in all things South American. Under Spanish rule, Peru was a vice royalty, and all South American colonies subject to it. The Chilenos, from environment, were a fighting race. The Araucanian Indians were the most war-like Indians of the continent, claiming to have ever remained unconquered. The whites [in Chile] had perpetual war [with the Araucanians], and have had almost the same with Peru. The Chilenos are intensely patriotic, and the cosmopolitan populations are united in their adoption of action and condition. The most popular here was Bernardo O'Higgins, who has a heroic statue erected in his memory.

Chile has pushed its frontiers north and south with a treaty of the newer nation, Argentina, of perpetual peace and arbitration, with a statue of Christ on the boundary in the Andes, dedicated with religious ceremonies and inscription. The treaty has been obeyed. The most southern city of the world, Punta Arenas in the Straits of Magellan, is a Chileno city. The frontiers extend through Patagonia and Tierra Del Fuego, which by exploration has proved to be the "Emerald Isle" of the south, with great resources of pasturage and sheep raising, and forests of value. Southern Chile is the home of the edible apple; a tribe of Indians are called "the apple eaters." The varieties we know have been introduced and are flourishing as the finest in the world.

South America is said to be without coal or iron, although Chile, if I am not mistaken, has both, and I have recently read of immense iron deposits, "a Mesabi range"[8] in Brazil. The continent from Cape Horn to the Caribbean Sea is unbrokenly productive, equaled by none on earth.

We live in the age of coal and iron, and the rule of life is to utilize the raw products of the earth. The dawn of a new era of synthetic chemistry, when by electric energy all substances, our foods, fertilizers,

---

[7] The campers' practice of sharing sleep space for increased warmth.

[8] Mesabi Range is the largest of three iron ranges in Minnesota.

clothing, our dwellings cooled and heated, metals unknown to the ancients, are procured or utilized by electric heat of uniform intensity and control, impossible to be done with burning coal. I saw a recent notice of aluminum being treated so as to be superior to steel in utility and temper. When the vision someone has seen of the New Zealander pondering the strange ruins on the banks of the Thames,[9] of the people lost in the mists of antiquity, the builders of the ruins, it will be the South American. It's a region in which everything grown on this planet flourishes within abundance unknown elsewhere, with power unlimited by electric energy.

The continent, being situated between two oceans, is subject to the trade winds produced by solar heat and the revolution of the earth to the eastward, to meet the water-laden atmosphere flowing over the continent to the mighty range of the Andes arrested by the high, cold summits, condensed in rain on the vast area to the eastward, being the richest and best water for agriculture on earth. The narrow strip some one hundred miles wide on the Pacific side, from sea level to a summit of some twenty thousand or more feet, with a short and rapid stream and their uniform flow from the perpetual unchanging heat of the tropics. The power of electric energy thus produced is beyond the imagination of man and quantity and uniformity.

---

[9] From Thomas Macaulay's essay, "On Ranck's 'History of the Popes'": "And she may still exist in undiminished vigour when some traveller from New Zealand shall, in the midst of a vast solitude, take his stand on a broken arch of London Bridge to sketch the ruins of St. Paul's." Gustave Doré created an engraving, "Where London Stood," that accompanied a related essay by Blanchard Jerrold; see http://traumwerk.stanford.edu:3455/71/47.

5. Coming to San Francisco

AT VALPARAISO WE GOT material for repair of damages made by the storms between Rio de Janeiro and Cape Horn, and our ship carpenter made good. We had made forty days between New York and Rio, and the same from there to Valparaiso, and looked for about the same from there to San Francisco. We did not make it. We made it in sixty days. We were four days at Rio and six at Valparaiso, or 170 days in all.

Our voyage from Valparaiso was uneventful. We sighted at a distance the island of St Felix and Ambrose off the coast of Peru, but no other land. When we crossed the equator and northerly to the latitude from Panama, we were about a thousand miles from land. For about one week we were in a dead calm, in a glassy sea, our ship "like a painted ship on a painted ocean,"[10] our shadows the size of our shoulders and hat brim, the heat intense, the pitch frying out of the deck seams.

We amused ourselves by fishing for sharks, with a strong hook and a small chain attached, baited with pork. We would cut them up to see if we could find the remains of anyone they had eaten or of gold watches or rings we have read of, but found none. Sometimes we found sharks in embryo, proving they were not produced from eggs.[11] I do not know whether all deep sea fish are produced that way. We swimmers would get permits from the captain for a boat, would row some miles, and would go in swimming. It was something to think of the unfathomable depths beneath us.

---

[10] Samuel Taylor Coleridge, "The Rime of the Ancient Mariner":
Day after day, day after day,
We stuck, nor breath nor motion;
As idle as a painted ship
Upon a painted ocean.
Water, water, every where,
And all the boards did shrink;
Water, water, every where,
Nor any drop to drink.

[11] From the Smithsonian Institute Ocean Portal: "Sharks have young in three different ways. After internal fertilization, some species lay a thick egg case that encloses the shark embryo (seen in the photo here). Most species are ovoviviparous, which means that the shark hatches and develops within the female shark and is born live. A third way (viviparous) is similar to human development, where the young shark grows within the female and gets nutrients from a placental link to the mother." See http://ocean.si.edu/ocean-photos/shark-embryo.

It was a tedious time. Character came out in the passengers, the worst and the best. Stealing from the ship's provisions was all right—it was our due—but from one another was unendurable. I laid in some stores of nuts, dried fruits, and so on at Valparaiso. Everything was stolen. As an old gardener from Mississippi said, "They would steal a sick nigger's medicine."

Before we arrived at San Francisco, I had a kind of ship's fever, leaving me very weak, just able to walk. As I have said, I had no connection with anyone onboard, most of whom were in companies. I had formed friendships with some good men from Dutchess County, New York; and the nearest friend from home was Philo S. Woodin[12] of Sherman and Egbert Luddington[13] of Quaker Hill, comparatively old men, but good men and true.

As soon as the anchor was down, our connection as passengers closed. The ship was bound for China, and the sailors immediately commenced smashing bunks and all conveniences. The cooks stopped their labors and we were hustled. The word was, "Get your traps and go ashore."

Ashore in San Francisco

SAN FRANCISCO FACES THE east on the hillside of the promontory between the bay and the ocean. It was a city of tents and light materials, and a few old adobe houses, with the nucleus around Portsmouth Square. My friends helped me with all kindness to go with them as they had a tent which they pitched like hundreds of others. The ships were coming loaded with passengers. The principle was "the devil take the hindmost."

The reaction from the sea voyage, change from sea-food, and the motion of the ship brought on enteric disease. San Francisco was a hell of pestilence and vice. People were dying by hundreds and were buried without ceremony. I was immediately taken in my weak state with the prevalent disease.

Of course, the first thing everyone did was to go to the post office. There were two delivery places, from "A" to "K" and from "K" to "Z."

---

[12] Cited as the husband of Mary in the Lanesville, Litchfield County, CT cemetery records. See http://dunhamwilcox.net/ct/lanesville_cem.htm.

[13] Cited in the Luddington-Saltus Records Pawling, Dutchess County, NY records. See http://www.jenforum.org/luddington/messages/6.html.

I was in the line waiting for my turn. There was a blazing flash before me. I was conscious of falling and knew no more. How long I lay there I knew not. No one noticed me. I became conscious got up, and managed to get back to the tent of my friends. One of the doctors of the ship we came in was nearby; he prescribed with no appreciable benefit. I felt I was going. My life was saved by a letter.

There were three young men, I being the youngest, who were of similar conditions of life. We each had everything to gain and nothing to lose but our lives and, by realizing all our resources, could go to California. We expected to go together: Benjamin Buckingham, my cousin, and James Richards, not a relative. We were much attached. We were "Ben, Jim, and Ralph." They could make their resources available without delay; I could not.

They joined a company that chartered a vessel for the Rio Grande River between Texas and Mexico. They went up the river to Monterey, thence across the battlefield of Buena Vista, through Durango [Mexico] to Mazatlán, and thence up to California, arriving in May, having started in January. Jim—with two others of the party, one being a carpenter as Jim also was—not being successful in the mines, returned to San Francisco to work at his trade, with promising results. On my getting my means available, I started alone around Cape Horn to join them. I wrote to Jim when I was ready to sail, informing him of conditions and the ship I was coming in.

Jim died and was buried the day I arrived.

W. Watson, his friend and associate of the party he came with, found among his affects my letter and in the newspaper the arrival of the ship *Samoset*. He put a letter in the post office as to where he could be found. My friends brought the letter to me, and I sent them to find Watson. He came. I had known him at home; he was much older than I, a father of a family. I was to find him the kindest man living.

He said, "You will die here. Go with me to my boarding house. You can get a board at twenty-eight dollars a week and put yourself under the care of Dr. Turner of the United State Army." Watson had had the disease himself, but it had assumed a chronic form and he was convalescent.

With the assistance of my friends, I went. We had become much attached, and they manifested it at parting. They had found a sea captain of their acquaintance, and they embarked for the mines. Dr.

I: Going to California

Turner in his rounds, a spare man, stern looking, and absorbed in his profession, came at full speed on his bronco, wearing the uniform of the U.S. Army. Watson brought him to me. My money was going and I felt desperate, seeing the dead men carried by continually.

I said, "Doctor, this is no place for an ill-gathering sick man. If I am to die, say so, and let me alone. I will take it."

He examined me and said, "Young man, my patients don't all die. I should have saved Richards if I had been called in time. I understand this disease. I was with the Army through the Mexican War. Obey my orders and you will get well." He gave medicine and orders; he said "I will see you to-morrow," sprang on his bronco, and went in a cloud of dust. He gave me attention closely and in a few days I found myself in the hands of one who knew what to do and did it. The recovery was slow, and it seemed I would be without money and unable to work

In such contingency I thought to end it by burying myself in the harbor. I got a lesson in ethics which gave me a rule of action for life. A young man of my age and position was boarding there. One morning he didn't go to his breakfast at the bell call. Smith, the proprietor from Oregon, who came from the western states with a large family, thence down to California, said to him, "Breakfast is ready."

The young man did not start.

"Don't you feel as well as usual?"

He made no reply.

"What's the matter?"

"Mr. Smith, I have no more money and I am so weak I cannot work. I don't want to cheat you or beg. I don't know what to do."

"Young man, you will know more than you do now, some time. We are all liable to come to that. Go and get your breakfast and do so until you get well. You will come out of this and will get work, and pay me. But whether you do or not, I will trust you. Go in."

He went.

"Do to others what you would have them do to you, and ask of others and accept what you would give" is not an abstraction but scientific ethics.

I was impatient at my slow recovery and idleness and spoke to Dr. Turner about going to the mines. The next time he saw me, he said, "You are not strong enough to go to the mines yet. There will be a man to see you tomorrow morning who wants a man like you to do light work.

You will have better living than you can get at any boarding house. I have told him you are a Yankee and can do everything. He will give you one hundred dollars a month," and away he went at full speed as usual.

The man came, and I went there and found out that I could do the work, though very weak. I had good food and gained strength rapidly. My chief concern now was the payment of my doctor's bill. Dr. Turner had a younger man as partner, Dr. Coit of Massachusetts. They had invited me to come to their office, where they had books of miscellaneous kinds and acted like ministering angels generally, and in the midst of this pandemonium I found a resting place.

As I felt well now, I took what money I had left, went there, and said "Doctor, I would like my bill. I will pay you what money I have, and I will pay the rest as soon as I am able."

He took his book and pencil, figured and said, "Thirty-eight dollars."

"What?" I said in astonishment.

"Thirty-eight dollars," said he.

"Well, I can pay that. I supposed it would be at least two hundred dollars." I had about one hundred. I paid it and went back to my work.

Soon after I saw him on the nankeen bronco, always at full speed, coming down the hill.

"Here," he shouted, "Come here."

Well, I thought, he has found his mistake in that bill.

"Buckingham, I counted that money after you left and found you had paid me a dollar too much." He threw it to me and away he went.

To conclude this episode, when I had made arrangements to leave for the mines, I went to his office and said, "I am going to take the boat this afternoon for the mines. I want some medicine so if I have an attack of this disease I can take it."

"All right, I can fix some. Come up before you go and get it." I did so. The office was closed. In the entry on a table was a box of pills with my name on it with directions. I took it and left two dollars in its place. As I was about to step on the boat, Dr. Coit came up.

"So you're off. Good luck to you. You are a scholar and a gentleman. There are not ten men in San Francisco who would have left that money for that medicine."

As we shook hands, I was tearful and said I hoped he and Dr. Turner did not think I could be so ungrateful. I never saw them again. I heard of a Dr. Turner at a station in the Rocky Mountains, sometime afterwards. Should I see him when the time comes, when it is said to him, "In as much as ye have done it to one of the least of these my brethren, ye have done it unto me,"[14] I hope to step forward and say, "I am the one."

---

[14] Matthew 25:40.

II: Into California Gold Country

6. Up the Sacramento to the Stanislaus

I HAD SOLD ALL of my outfit I had brought from New York as soon as I was well enough to go aboard ship, which was cleared of all evidence of its former use. The captain and mate and some of the sailors stayed by her, enough to start on the voyage to China. The captain said he had heard I had been sick. I expressed my appreciation of his interest and said that I should always remember my voyage under Captain Hollis. I used to tease the master by my boyish deviltry but knew the limit, and he sometimes would call me Jonah and said he must pitch me overboard or the ship would never get through.

He replied to my parting words: "I shall remember, Jonah."

We shook hands and parted.

Watson had gone to the Sandwich Islands for a cargo of vegetables. I gave him my sea-chest and I left him my books, a journal I had kept. He came home soon afterwards. I was able to do him kindness in civilized life. When my youngest daughter was married, he was living in Kent with his wife, who was a school and church mate of my wife. There was a large company at our house of the best culture and intellectual life. I sent an invitation to them. They could go in any company and not be ashamed of or shame others. He spoke of the company as being above him. I threw my arm around his shoulders and said, "There is none here I would rather see than you; but for you there would be no wedding here today."

Leaving San Francisco

THE RAINY SEASON HAD come. On Montgomery Street[15], the water front then was a bottomless pit of mud with many carcasses of dead mules sticking in it. The beach had cargoes of Chileno flour stacked in sacks and all things perishable were destroyed. Flour went from ten cents to twenty cents one day.

I was reading [recently] of an excavation on the streets and the finding of a ship's hulk. I do not know how many streets have been built out on the water front, but several are founded on ships' hulks. I think there were at least one hundred ships at anchor in the bay with no one on board, being deserted as soon as the cargoes were landed. The ships were being towed ashore until they grounded at high tide; then they were surrounded with empty water casks fastened together and to the ship at low tide. At high tide, everything rose and was towed shoreward and grounded, and so on until beached, dismantled, made into storehouses and boarding houses, and buried as the city expanded into the harbor.

The ships were towed up the rivers to Sacramento and Stockton for that purpose (to be dismantled). We were on a sailboat, sloop-rigged, managed by two men. The boat was filled with boxes and barrels as high as the boom would swing, and on this cargo some dozen of us were perched, carrying our own provisions and blankets. No cooking on board and no place to lie down straight.

It rained every day and night. We went ashore at Benicia, sometime the capital of the territory and state, on the strait between San Francisco and Suisun Bay, which is the outlet of the Sacramento and San Joaquin rivers. Between the bays and the rivers is Monte Diavolo (Diablo; Devil's Mountain), forming the skyline of view from San Francisco eastward. The hillsides of Suisun Bay seem to be covered with snow, but it was the wild geese, migrated from the far north, wintering here.

The Tulare Plains is agricultural California, some six or seven hundred miles long, running from Sacramento on the north and San Joaquin on the south, bounded with the coast range of mountains and the Sierra Nevada on the east, some forty to sixty miles wide. It was

---

[15] Montgomery Street in San Francisco moved further from the shore during the gold rush years as the sandy bluffs near the waterfront were leveled and the shallows filled in. Before the infill, Montgomery Street was about seven blocks closer to the water than it is now.

II: Into California Gold Country

once an inland sea; the erosion of countless ages, principally from the Sierra Nevada, has made land. About seventy miles from the mouths of these rivers, Sacramento on the north and Stockton on the south, is a swamp with no trees, covered with a species of bull-rush some three to five feet high, called Tulles, waving like water in the wind. It is being reclaimed by dykes, the restored fertility of ages producing great crops, inexhaustibly fertile.

There were no landing places on the rivers below Sacramento on the north and Stockton on the south. The feeders of the San Joaquin were, commencing at the mouth, Cosumnes, Mokelumne, Calaveras, Stanislaus, Tuolumne, Mariposa, Mercedes and Kings' River, the Sacramento, the American, the Feather, and the Yuba. On these flowing westward, in the foothills between mountain and plain, some thirty miles wide, was the gold region of California.

Towards the head of the Sacramento, this gold region crossed the valley to the coast range and the drainage of the Klamath, equal in volume to the Sacramento or the San Joaquin, but a rapid stream with no harbor at its mouth, emptying directly into the ocean. Mt. Shasta, then thought the highest in the United States, was in the range. The gold region extended into the Oregon country.

I was bound for the Stanislaus and tributaries, where I had been informed Ben was. He had not heard from me. We were one week on the boat, it raining every day until we arrived at Stockton, the supply place for the southern mines. There the reports of the probability of starvation was such that but one of the party and myself, bound for the Mariposa, proceeded.

I found a mule train bound for the Stanislaus, chartered by a young man by the name of Pinto. He had been an officer in the Army in Mexico, was at the storming of Chapultepec. Several years ago I read of General Francis E. Pinto[16] of the Civil War being a resident of Brooklyn. I wrote him at Brooklyn to see if he was the man I made the contract with to carry my traps from Stockton to the mines. He replied he was the man, and gave me an account of his life as I did mine.

The season was closed for transportation by wagons, but Pinto saw money in it if he could get through with goods. It was some seventy miles.

---

[16] See General Pinto's biography at http://www.all-biographies.com/soldiers/francis_e_pinto.htm.

The trail over the plains was not thoroughly soaked, but where not packed by travel, the trail was bottomless mud; the most adhesive mud imaginable. A mule would sink to its body, then we'd unpack it, carry the pack to solid ground, roll the mule there, and pack again. The adjusting of the pack is a science. By that time another mule will be stuck. Sometimes it will take a month to get through, at a cost of fifty cents to a dollar a pound. The necessary profanity of mule drivers is well known. I could only imagine the language from the gestures of the Mexicans.

I kept company with the train for a few days. At night I cut some small brush, lay on the ground on mud, wrapped myself in my blanket and essayed to sleep; but I was not successful at first, with the streams of cold water percolating across my body from the rain.

At the ferry of the Calaveras, I left and let out for Carson's Creek on the Stanislaus, some forty miles away. I went thirty miles the first day, crossing the north and south forks of the Calaveras, by stripping and carrying my clothes over my head through the snow-cold waters from the mountains, then dressing and on again, arriving at the creek one morning, drenched and weary. I found a miner who had managed to make a fire and was cooking breakfast. I asked where I could get something to eat. He pointed to a place where he said there was a butcher who had meat.

"Do you know anyone by the name of Buckingham on this creek?" I asked.

"Yes," he pointed. "He is down there in that tent."

I went and pulled aside the curtain. There was Ben with his partner getting out of his blankets. With a yell I was pulled in. After a separation of ten months, we were together and never separated again as long as he stayed in the country. I was hustled into dry clothes and a dry blanket after two weeks' drenching and a wet blanket. They managed to make a fire, and with a hot stew and a cup of hot tea, the best drink in the world for a tired man, I was in the kingdom of heaven among ministering angels.

II: Into California Gold Country

7. The Mining Camp on Carson's Creek

BEN, I FOUND, HAD three partners. They had goods from San Francisco, intending to start a trading store. The goods had arrived piled up, covered with sailcloth. The house must be built. They offered employment to me. Ben and I were expert with axes, could chop, hew, split, and rive, and we went in. This was on Carson's Creek, a branch of the Stanislaus, named from Jim Carson, the brother of Kit Carson, the guide of Fremont. I had the money I had earned in San Francisco left, so I was square with the world upon arrival.

Origin of Gold and Visible Indications of Probabilities

WE MUST GO BACK in the geological ages to the time of the wrinkling of the earth's surface by shrinking, as on the moon's surface, where there is no erosion. In this portion of the hemisphere, scientists say there was a glacial age of ice about a mile in thickness. With the infinitely slow, perpetual movements grinding and transporting earth and rocks, we find smooth stones almost everywhere, with boulders many tons in weight, ledges cropping out, hundreds of feet in depth in others.

The indications in California are different. It is the land of earthquakes and erosion of water, by which mountains were brought low and valleys were filled. The great central I have spoken of, filled with erosion principally from the Sierra Nevada ("mountains of snow"). The most striking proof of erosion in its magnitude I ever saw is Table Mountain between Stanislaus and Tuolumne Rivers. As you rise to the divide of the Calaveras and look across the canon of the Stanislaus, the skyline of mountains seems of water level and smoothness. It was once a river bed. By volcanic action in the Sierra Nevadas, basaltic lava poured down, filling the valley and changing the river beds of the Stanislaus and Tuolumne. By the erosion of countless ages, this river bed filled with rock commonly called "trap," the least erosive known. It became a mountain several hundred feet higher than the present rivers divide between them. A gold bearing strata was found under this ridge by tunneling.

Wherever there was smooth stones indicating erosion, there gold might be found. The matrix of gold is quartz or silica rock, one of the igneous or primary rocks bursting through the slate or secondary rocks; the strata standing at various degrees of inclination, and the erosion of slate and quartz bearing the gold in the rough nearest to the matrix in pebbles or nuggets, according to distance. Fine gold is more generally disseminated, as on the banks or beds now existing or on old river beds where changed by earthquakes or by volcanic action.

The gold-bearing rock had considerable iron in sulphuric form, as had also the stratified overlying rock crystallized in squares (we called them "fairy brick"). When washing, the heaviest remains with black sand; iron could be removed by a magnet. This iron in the soil made a reddish tinge.

An Aside: Placer Miners

IT IS NOT COMMONLY known that Australian gold was discovered by Californians. In the party I have spoken of, and of which Ben was a member, was a boy in his teens by name of Morehouse. On arrival in California he drifted to parts unknown and was not heard from for many years. On my return, his father spoke to me of him probably being dead.

I replied, "Not necessarily. I had known men well who had no name apparently, called Oregon, Texas Bill, Nick of the Woods, or Rocky Mountain Charlie, and so on. You may never hear from him. Still he may be alive."

The father died. After some ten or twelve years, the son wrote home and finally came, his family broken up. He came to see me and said, "I was at work on Wood Creek, a branch of the Tuolumne, one of the first working in the southern mines. I had as partner some Australians, one named Hargreaves who said, 'I believe there is gold in Australia. There is a country there that looks like this, the soil and rocks. I am going back and prospect it!' So I went with them. We discovered gold, but were not fortunate in making a strike. Finally I came back to California."

After I saw him, Morehouse went west and into oblivion, like hundreds of thousands of others.

Not ten percent of placer miners ever advanced their fortune by digging gold. Their expenses ate it up. The original deposit, the primeval erosion, was greater when there was little obstruction to the flow of water, the rocks nearly bare as indicated by the large stones in it. After

deposits were sought after—sometimes little covering of earth, sometimes several feet in depth—no indications remain on the surface of where the original water course was. I have frequently had claims valueless alongside others of hundreds of thousands in value.

Fabulous sums have been reported of strikes; many men I have known of made hundreds of dollars, some of thousands. The most I ever knew of was a man who came into the mines, took up a claim some fifteen feet in diameter, dug out some six thousand dollars in a few weeks, went down to San Francisco and reported; he said any man who knew what he was about could make it. Consequently, all clerks, waiters, and transients made a rush, became dead broke, and went into the debris.

Camp Government

AS CONDITIONS DEMANDED, THE mining camps formed a government. The Alcalde (a magistrate) and a sheriff were elected, who decide the differences about claims and tried criminals when called upon, although the law was indefinite. Generally each one's law was "to right his wrongs when they were given."

We had a case in camp. An Irishman got drunk. His bag of gold was gone when he got sober. Some specimens, curious pieces he had shown, where offered in trade by one of the camp, thus identifying the thief. The sheriff arrested him. A jury was summoned, I being one. The Alcalde opened court on the head of a flour barrel. Jim Smith, a lawyer from Philadelphia, was appointed council for the prisoner. The Irishman swore to the theft of the pieces of gold. His evidence was sustained.

The case was so clear that an old sailor, a mate of the ship, had prepared a cat-o-nine-tails. The court sentenced the prisoner at the "bar"-rel to have his shirt taken off, arms tied around a tree, and three strokes given by thirteen men, then banished or shot by anyone upon his appearance in camp. When he had been given thirty lashes by us, his back was so bad that by unanimous consent he was cut down, his shirt given him, and he departed with the warning aforesaid.

ಒ

THE FOLLOWING IS AN episode of my own. Sometime afterwards when the store was in operation, a big fellow by the name of Tripp, who had been a whale-man, one of the minor officers onboard ship, a jolly good fellow. I had worked with him. He came into the store, some drunk. One of the party accused him of stealing a canister of powder. Tripp became furious and declared he would shoot anyone who called him a thief. The accuser, inclined to bluster but a coward at heart, screamed with terror when he could have protected himself, having pistols within reach. With the assistance of Daggett of Maine, who had been first mate of a whale ship, we got Tripp out. By that time, Tripp, foaming with passion, knew neither friends or foe, declared with rifle cocked that he would kill anyone who touched him. I told Daggett that Tripp was more in danger than anyone else, as he was so crazy his rifle would go off, and then someone would shoot him.

"We had better take his rifle away from him."

"Yes," says he, "but rather a ticklish job for us though."

Says I, "I think we can do it. Tripp is a good fellow. I'll get as near to him as I can by talking to him and when I give the word, spring in and grasp the rifle."

I approached him. "Tripp, you know I'm your friend, how we worked together on the Stanislaus, how we used to lie in the tent when it rained, and you taught me how to play 'Old Sledge'[17] at cards."

"I know, but you keep back. I'll shoot you as soon as anyone."

As I approached, he started to raise his gun. I gave a yell at Daggett, and I sprung in. I caught the muzzle of the rifle, Daggett the breech. Tripp was the most powerful man I ever encountered. He wore a number twelve miner's boot. He kicked me in the side, nearly knocking me out. He kicked again. I caught his foot, took a hip lock, and threw him. Daggett wrung his rifle away and ran with it. I let up. His anger was indescribable. He would kill me on sight whenever he saw me. I laughed at him, saying we were good friends now as we always should be. I saw no more of him for several months. I was working several miles from there, alone at a hole, the earth about even with my head. I heard a step and, looking up, there stood Tripp. He was out prospecting and looked like a walking arsenal. With rifles, pistols, and Bowie knife in belt. In a flash there came to me our last interview and his threats. I jumped from the hole and grasped his hands, "Hello, Tripp. I'm glad

---

[17] A card game; also called All Fours, High-Low-Hack or Seven Up. See http://en.wikipedia.org/wiki/All_Fours.

to see you." He responded. We talked of our luck like friends. Tripp says, "I don't know when we shall meet again."

There was a Mexican store nearby. "Let us go up to the Mexicans and have some wine."

"Of course we will," I said.

We went, chinked our glasses in friendship and good luck, and parted. I never saw him again, but I heard he had an unforgivable grudge against my camp mate for his accusation of theft.

Of a different case was the "bad man" one sometimes meets. Archibald Osborn of Arkansas was one. He was with a party of Texans. They called him in their playful language "that ——— Arkansas hoss thief." When he was drunk he was dangerous. There was a man from Massachusetts named Howard, a reserved, gentlemanly fellow who came into the store where Arch was drunk and quarreling. He made approaches to Howard, who pushed him aside. Arch attacked him. Howard set his jaw and squared himself.

One of Ben's partners was Sam Whitton of Massachusetts. A good fellow was Sam; he was a stalwart machinist, had worked at the Springfield Armory,[18] and was the best rifle shot I ever saw. His business in the Armory was sighting of the rifles. He had tools and all came to him for repairs of firearms. As Arch came up, Howard took him a sock under one ear that sent him over into the corner among Sam's tools. Arch fell where there was some rock drills: steel bars, two feet long. He caught one and came for Howard, who screamed with terror. Sam and I sprung in for Arch. I caught the drill and wrung it from him, and Sam put Arch out as an unfair fighter, he breathing and threatening slaughter.

Howard said, "I am a peaceable man. He has gone for his pistol to shoot me. I demand your protection."

Sam says, "He won't come through that door with a pistol."

Arch didn't come back.

Sometime afterwards there was an election. We had several: one for territorial legislature, one for Constitutional convention, one for adoption of a Constitution, and so on. The election was held in the trading store of an Englishman named Reed. Ben and I had been out at work all day. In the evening I went over to see what was going on. As I went

---

[18] A national historic site. See http://www.nps.gov/spar/historyculture/sa-woodworking.htm.

in, I saw the room full of roughs, roaring drunk, with Arch and my friend Daggett as leaders. It was pandemonium sure. Arch saw and made for me. Immediately I was the drunkest and roughest of that crowd. With a lurch I came against Arch with an impact which nearly upset him.

"Hello, Old Arch," as I clung to him for support, "what will you have to drink? Come boys," as I staggered to the bar, "Choose yer Pizen."

As the crowd came up, I heard someone say, "I never saw him drunk before."

I said, "I have all I can stand under. Give me some beer."

As they were drinking, I staggered to the door and, as soon as through, put for camp and told Ben of my escape. The next day I went to settle with Reed, his account several times more than real. I looked at him but said nothing. My playing drunk was costly. I said to Daggett soon afterwards, "What did it cost you, that spree at Reed's?"

He looked serious. "The damnest bill you ever saw."

"I thought so," I said, "when I paid mine."

Daggett said, "I never saw you drunk before."

I said, "Honor bright now, you shall not tell of it. I never was drunk in my life and had not drank a drop then. I saw there was a prospect of a row with Arch where one of us might be killed, and I took that way out of it."

8. Ben, Phillips, and the Working Company

WE WERE LIVING AN expensive life. No food cost less than one dollar per pound. Ben and I were at work at the Stanislaus, living in a small tent, so rainy that we had to watch our chances to cook for everything was wet. Ben was ill. I said to him, "I will go up to the ferry and get you a dry shirt and a dose of castor oil."

I paid eight dollars for the shirt and three dollars for the oil.

The express came in from San Francisco, bringing the mail. I had three most-welcome letters in return from those I had sent from Rio, Valparaiso, and San Francisco. I paid ten dollars and fifty cents for them. New York papers, one dollar each.

II: Into California Gold Country

I offered sixteen dollars to a Frenchman for his shovel. He replied, "No." I sent by express to San Francisco for two, which cost twenty-eight dollars.

As spring opened, the rains ceased, with no rain from the first of April to the first of November. The plains and the foothills were covered with flowers, the old oak trees—the slow growth of centuries—giving a park-like look, as beautiful as the imagination could conceive. The country had been well prospected, and no new region on the gold-bearing land could be discovered.

One other creek, known as Six Mile Creek, had two branches, both having been worked. Where they came together was a deep place which had not been worked. It was confidently believed there was a rich deposit in it, and one old miner who had worked there said, "There is a bushel of gold in there."

So we formed a company to work it, of various conditions of men.

Daggett was the Down East whale man.

James M.B. Smith was of the aristocracy of Philadelphia, graduate of Princeton College, a lawyer; he had a law office with Phillip Dallas, son of the vice president.

Hall, an English Naval Officer, had served in the East Indies under Sir Edward Belcher[19] (the Lord Edward of Marryatt's Naval Officer) in charting, surveying, and exterminating Malay Pirates. Hall told us of Queen Victoria. (When she died, anecdotes were published of her. I sent a story of his to the *New York Times*, warranted "never seen in print." My nephew, a New York merchant, sent it to a friend in England, said it would be seen by King Edward.)

Hyde was an officer in the English Army.

Murray, a Scotch-Irishman, had been a sailor and a soldier, had deserted for Newfoundland, and got into Boston. The next morning he found himself in the streets with shirt and pants, enlisted in the Navy under Commodore Stockton[20]. He came around Cape Horn, was with the squadron when California was annexed, and deserted at Mazatlán, Mexico. Murray got to California on discovery of gold on the

---

[19] Admiral Belcher was a naval surveyor and Arctic expedition leader. See http://en.wikipedia.org/wiki/Edward_Belcher

[20] Robert Stockton, a U.S. naval commodore who participated in the capture of California in the Mexican-American war. See http://en.wikipedia.org/wiki/Robert_F._Stockton.

American River, and was lucky. A man told me he knew of his coming in there three times with ten pounds of gold, two thousand each time, which lasted him not more than two weeks.

Said I, "How do you make such lucky strikes, Murray?"

"Well, when I get over a 'bust,' I go out, take off my hat where there are no indications, swing it three times around my head and throw it. Where it strikes, I dig and strike."

And there was Ben, his partner, and myself. The firm of Ben and company had dissolved down to two with some little profit and a lot of debts, most of which were uncollectable. We had a meeting. Nothing in writing, no security possible. Daggett, the sailor, was appointed captain; I, the youngest, was appointed treasurer. Hall, the naval officer, was appointed caterer. Each man served a day as cook in rotation.

We cut a channel through the rock and drained the premises partly. We made a large pump with two men's power necessary to use it. After several months working, making less than expense, one after another left, leaving Ben and me to close the concern and pay the indebtedness. Ben and his partner, having financed the concern in the beginning, and I as treasurer must see the thing through. Ben's partner, seeing the failure and prospect, shirked and formed a new partnership, so that we had nothing left but our honor.

The other members of the party led loose lives, addicted to sensuality, would pay a debt if convenient, if not would shirk it on the whole good-hearted fellows, had no belief in my purity of ideals, had respect for my recklessness of odds in a contest. Altogether they left with friendly feelings for Ben and me.

With us it was different. Our salvation was in results from our labor. Ben, before I met up him, had some success but not enough to warrant him to return home. He was the youngest of five brothers, living with his mother and a widowed sister with a child, the paternal estate undivided. His bachelor brother advanced on Ben's signature an amount to give him an outfit for California. There was a girl "who might have been," but he could not take her to the ancestral home under the conditions. There was no pledge but some understanding, dependent on the future. He was some four years older than me.

With me, the case was different. There was a girl in this case. I was twenty-one years old. She was some four years younger. I was a younger son through several generations. Her ancestry was some higher than mine. Her grandfather had been M.C., a candidate for governor of the state. Her father was educated at West Point, one of the most brilliant men of the town; her brother, the only son, was attached to my sister and my dear friend, a kindred spirits next to my own heart. I thought indications favorable. Her parents treated me kindly, particularly her father. After I had engaged my passage, I went to see her. I told her my hopes. The response was all I desired. We would wait and hope. She said her mother would object to correspondence, but we were pledged. I had formed my ideals from Sir Walter Scott's novels and longed for the joys of battle and results. The joy of battle I had, but no result to warrant my return. The agony of failure; the collapse of the bridge connecting the past and the future seemed inevitable. I had no distraction of society, while I saw the absence must be effectual with her in the society she was encompassed with, and I should give place to a memory becoming dim. In honor, I must not move. This is ancient history. The actors gone over the river long since. I wait for the boat.

☙

ONE OF THE MOST influential partners I had subsequently was only Phillips, a native of Providence, Rhode Island. He was a blacksmith on a whale ship, had left the ship at Valparaiso, been on a steamer between that port and Callao, the seaport of Lima, had been in South America eleven years. Some years older than I, the man had the most physical endurance I ever met, and was a total abstainer from intoxicating drinks.

At one time, Chile and Peru being at war, the Peruvian fleet was expecting to bombard Valparaiso; the commandant wanted gun carriages ironed in haste. Phillips, with his native helpers, took the contract. The work was satisfactorily done in time, to the envy of the other blacksmiths who, as Phillips said, all drank, thinking as many do, that the necessity of the work demanded it. So he challenged all South America on a bet of one thousand dollars for a contest of heavy work on time. No one took it, and no one who drank could stand a tramp with him.

"Of course, they can't do it; they drink."

After a tramp with him over the mountains for forty miles one day, I said, "Phillips, I can't walk with you. I can with anyone else."

"Pshaw! You can walk as well as I can."

"I cannot. You don't know how tired I get."
"Don't you suppose I ever get tired?"
"I never saw you tired."
"I don't always say I am."

It was enough. I never said I was tired again. It was thought we were indivisible.

Phillips and Ben's former partner had been at work somewhere and had made good. They had worked out their claim at Carson's. We were evidently going back to where they had been, and we were not going to let anyone know it. They were our camp mates, and we were not going to be left. Finally Phillips said, "We will give you ten dollars a day for two weeks, and then you can go on your own."

"All right, we'll do it."

When anyone started for new diggings, they generally went in the night as they had their gold on their persons, having kept it buried, so we were to take a midnight walk. We got everything ready, and after the lights went out, took our packs and stole away. Phillips said it was about ten miles, a trail most of the way. He went ahead, keeping to the trail, a beaten path, by the feel of his feet; we followed like wise. Finally he said, "We were about here."

We went along a steep hillside until he said that there was a good place to unpack. Our feet encountered camp tools and cooking ware, which went rattle bang down to the creek.

Voices in alarm shouted, "¿Quién es?" ("Who goes there?")

Phillips was at home in Spanish and replied, "*Los Patriotas*." ["The patriots"]

We had come onto a camp of Mexicans in the darkness.

We went a short distance, laid down our packs, and got into our blankets. They, very foolishly, got up and built a fire to light the surroundings and watch for the rest of the night, not thinking that if anyone wanted to attack them, the light would make the aim sure. Ben, after a while, got up thirsty and crept down to the water. As he was climbing up the bank, they saw and fired at him. The charge went over his head.

"Fire away!" shouted Ben. They were surprised the next morning to see us get up out of the grass a few rods away.

When Phillips had gone away, he had buried his gold in a leather bag, taking sights from familiar objects to make lines, and where the lines crossed, there he made a deposit. He went out there and looked, and found there a camp fire exactly over his gold. He went with his shovel, cleaned their fire away, and dug up the deposit. The bag had been destroyed by the heat. He shoved it into his pan and went to the creek to wash it out. The Mexicans looked on in speechless astonishment, he bantering them about their knowledge of gold digging.

"Suppose they could smell it?" we asked.

"O! They would not have taken it. It was not theirs," Phillips said.

I had yet to learn their respect for the property of others. We worked as agreed on an unworked portion of the creek, believing there was connection of working above and below. We did not strike the lead, but made enough so that they did not lose by hiring us; so they left the claim.

I told Ben I thought the oldest deposit was on the other side of the creek. We worked there and found it. We had been together about a year then. It was no great strike, but we made some one thousand dollars each in a short time, and began to see light. This was in the dry season, so we threw up the paying earth on the bank to wash when the rains came, picking out the visible pieces. We had several workings some distance apart where we piled up the pay earth.

The rainy season approaching, we sent Phillips to San Francisco for our winter supplies and his partner. Ben and I built a house, avoiding some of the errors of the winter before, and made ourselves comfortable in dry quarters.

9. Vigilance Committee Times

THE PIONEERS OR IMMIGRANTS were generally of a high type. They were of the class who had some capital, or a character that could command some. But many failed, especially those inclined to gamble. They would go to a city where a cart load of silver and gold would be displayed. What they had would seem so little and the chance of doubling it indefinite, so apparent they would test it and of course be cleaned out.

Phillips, with his South American experience, explained the tricks of the games and the command they had of conditions. so that one who made a stake would win or lose at their will. They would be drawn on until they were cleaned out. It was said that the gambler would never reform. He would rob or murder, but never work again. There were many who had been convicts from Australia, and at one time the city of San Francisco was at their mercy. The authorities were in league and connived at or condoned the crime. This was the vigilance committee times.

A witness told me of a sight when five hundred men marched through the street with a revolver in hand, twelve abreast, up to the prison, took up the robbers, murderers, and gamblers, and hung them. This made an exodus to the mines, where the process was repeated. The small party of Mexicans we came in contact with were the advance guard of many more. A village was the consequence nearby, the vilest of both sexes living like beasts of prey and entitled to the same consideration. American gamblers, Mexican thieves, and vile women.

Sunday was a general day when life could be seen; the Mexican dress was a gay-colored serape or long blanket, a loose-sleeved shirt, and pants open at the side, buttoned partly, the white drawers beneath. Watch them carefully. Their hands hung at their sides. The knife handle held by the two fingers up their sleeves, the blade one foot long. When wanted, the knife was out like a flash. The serape would be wound around the left arm and used as a guard, the right hand with the knife, and they went in. Of course, they were no match for the American gamblers with their revolvers.

One night they had a row. Four Mexicans were killed. One gambler I saw when the surgeon came to sew him up; he had a cut across his face diagonally, one eye destroyed. We did not interfere. The more gamblers killed the better.

As I said, Ben and I had a large quantity of pay earth heaped up, waiting for water, which did not come until near spring. The Mexicans were of all grades of blood, from pure Spanish to pure Mexican; the *padrones* more Spanish; the peons held in semi-slavery, more Indian. The *padrones* would send the peons out into the diggings, and they would steal our pay earth, carry it away or work it dry and get enough to make it profitable to the *padrones*. Their village was between us and the pay earth. We would go to look about, and as soon as we left, the Mexicans would go in and steal.

I said, "Ben, I will catch those fellows tomorrow."

So early in the morning I started in the opposite direction until I was out of sight, took a turn around the mountain, and found a place and concealed myself. I had a double-barreled gun loaded with shot, a pistol with balls, and a good Bowie knife. I would give them shot first, then if necessary, pistols and knife in close quarters. Soon some dozen of them came up, looked around and, seeing nothing, began to scrape the earth into their bowls. I stepped out and shot. He had a thick coat on or I should have killed him, being close enough, I think. They broke and ran for camp without looking back. I loaded up and waited, but there was no return.

I took his tools and went for their camp. A meat trader I had traded with pointed out to me their tent, a gambling place where they had gone in. With my gun cocked, I went in, the *padrone* being present. I passed the tools to the one I had shot. I stepped back so no one could get behind me. I had a few words of Spanish, so I could use them. The *padrone* asked me if I had come to fight.

"Si."

I gave them illustrated English and Spanish. They knew several would die before I did and did not attack me. I told them I never would use small shot again. I departed, keeping my eye out, so they could not strike me in the back.

The next day I went through the village to the diggings. They had not been back. There was an M.D., an educated Cherokee Indian, who would be taken for a white man. As I passed he said to me, "There was a Mexican shot above here yesterday."

"Was he hurt much?" I said.

"Well, he had a thick coat on and that saved him. I got some twenty-six shot out of him, some he will keep."

41

I did not tell him what I knew about it. That nightfall we heard up and down the creek: "Where is the man who shot the Mexican?"

There were some Canadians, Bob and Joe Hamilton. Their father founded the city of Hamilton, on the railroad between Niagara and Detroit. There were some glorious good fellows from New Hampshire and Massachusetts, each with a bottle of wine.

"Where is the man who shot the Mexican?" was the cry.

They found him.

It averaged about a murder a week within hearing distance. Some were hung a few miles away. I was not there. Ben and I were quiet, peaceable men, and he had the confidence of our fellows. Some Massachusetts men had a dispute with one of our camp mates over a claim (we were not partners otherwise). They agreed to leave it to us as arbitrators. Our camp mate was not well liked by us, and he presumed on our connection to favor him. He was wrong, and we said so, much to his chagrin and to the satisfaction to those who knew of it besides the claimants, who were known as men who would neither do nor suffer injustice.

☙

PERHAPS WHAT I AM NOW to say should not be said, but this is a personal experience of educational influences. I had in "the baseless fabric of my visions,"[21] seen a strike of gold which I could use in education fitting me to take a position beside "the girl I left behind me," not doubting her affection, but with the uttermost of what I was capable of, I had failed to realize my ideal. The collapse came. I received a letter

---

[21] From Prospero's speech in Shakespeare's *Tempest*, Act IV, Scene i:
You do look, my son, in a moved sort,
As if you were dismay'd: be cheerful, sir.
Our revels now are ended. These our actors,
As I foretold you, were all spirits, and
Are melted into air, into thin air:
And, like the baseless fabric of this vision,
The cloud-capp'd towers, the gorgeous palaces,
The solemn temples, the great globe itself,
Yea, all which it inherit, shall dissolve,
And, like this insubstantial pageant faded,
Leave not a rack behind. We are such stuff
As dreams are made on; and our little life
Is rounded with a sleep.

from her; she had changed. It was young girl's fancy, and it passed with her environment. Not so with mine. I had not spoken to a woman for years; the vision of her was with me always. I had faced death in various forms by flood and field, and knew something of the sensations. The problem was not to face death but face life, the prospect a desert with a blazing sun, waterless, without shade, stretching in the distance. How easy to leave it.

As I went out from my camp mates to the great pine tree, I wrestled with the conditions. I had been trusted by her and her parents. No restraint had been put on my intercourse with her. My dearest male friend at home was her brother who was soon to wed my sister. He and my oldest brother were my principle correspondents by letter. There was no other way but to sink my own personality and leave no cloud on her memory. I wrote her that she had been always free and I exacted no pledge, and I would never remind her by word or act of my unfortunate love. Her brother was indignant at the breaking and wrote me accordingly. His and my sister's happiness was at stake. I wrote that if he had any friendship for me to show it by showing his sister an unabated affection. I would, as I wrote her, meet life as a man and in my humble way conduct myself so as not to shame them by their memory of me.

I have lived a life of self respect. No man, woman, or child has suffered wrong through a voluntary act of mine. The ills of life I was not equal to remove; I would bear to the death, which I courted. The intense feeling I experienced found a safety valve in language and action.

☙❧

PHILLIPS, WHOM I HAVE spoken of as my camp mate, said to me one day, "Did you have a row with that Canadian down the creek?"

"Why?" said I.

"That old fellow that worked near you said to me, 'Say now, ain't that little pard of yours considerable of a cuss? Can he fight as well as he can talk? The way that he went for that Canuck who meant to drive him out of his claim by building a dam and shutting off the water. He came up with his shovel tore up the dam, with his shovel up ready to split his head and pour out fire and brimstone in a way that beat me. I can cuss some myself but I never heard so much of it and in the same time as he gave it!"

I explained to Phillips, saying that I perhaps did let myself out some. The Canuck didn't repair his dam.

&

OUR ENVIRONMENT WAS STRENUOUS. One of my camp mates was an Englishmen, an inoffensive fellow. It was our entertainment to hear him spout Shakespeare. We called him Richard III. So when we were settled in the evening with the pipe of peace, we said, "Come, Dick, let's have some tragedy." He, nothing lost, would give it intensively. He went away on a prospecting tour, some forty miles to the Moquelemne[22]. He was gone several days. We found his body, a bullet through his head, lying on his blanket. Apparently he had laid down to rest on returning; his clothes were cut open in search for his belt.

Two men had a house not far away. A party of Mexicans rode up and dismounted for a light for their cigarettes. The householders were attacked. One sprang through the door and escaped, the other was stabbed and left for dead, the house ransacked. An old man, an American with his Spanish wife, found him and nursed him back to life. I saw him. Probably he would never get well. The old American had a home in Mexico; he said they were going back soon and would take him with them. Ben and I gave an ounce of gold to help; others did likewise.

&

ONE MORE EPISODE AND I will change the subject. The bad man: Sam had been in the army in the Mexican War. Many of the volunteers after the war came to California. Sam was usually a quiet fellow, but when in liquor was a terror; with his army rifle, he would shoot at a friend or a foe. Nearby was a store with a Frenchman, his Mexican wife and child, nearly two years old. The woman had the respect of all and was good to look at. (I had not seen a white child in the country.) Sam became intoxicated, went to the store-house, and attempted liberties with the woman. My work was nearby, and I saw it all. She complained to her husband. I called to his partner, "You had better take care of Sam."

"Oh, Sam won't do any hurt."

---

[22] Mokelumne, in Calaveras County, California.

II: Into California Gold Country

Sam came out loading his gun. The woman had a wagon, drawing her child. The Frenchmen ran in, fastening the door on my side, another door on the backside. Sam ran around, and I heard the door being smashed.

I ran around. As I passed the corner, I was looking into the muzzle of his cocked rifle, the woman holding the end of the barrel, the Frenchmen and Sam struggling at the breach. I caught the rifle, and they did me the honor to let go and leave me with Sam. Like a flash I wrung the rifle from him, fired it in the air. As he made advances, I told him in California English that if he made a step forward I should have killed him. He knew it and paused. His partners came up.

"Yes, Sam was going too far."

I kept his rifle, leaving them fighting on the grounds, hands locked in beards and hair. They finally got Sam into the house. Some hours afterwards, Sam came out repentant and sober, begged my pardon in tears.

"Will you give me my rifle?"

"Yes, and some advice with it. You know when you get drunk you are like a mad dog and should have the same treatment. If ever you get on another 'tear' on this creek, I swear I'll kill you if no one else does. Take notice."

He promised all kinds of goodness. All went quiet for nearly a month.

When we came in for our midday meal, word came that Sam had broken loose and shot at old Irish Andy. I went out and roused the camp and found a cattle lasso.

"Come boys, this has gone on long enough. Let's go down and finish Sam."

We went. His partners had disarmed him, and he was getting sober.

"Here," I said, "I said I would kill you. But we'll give you fifteen minutes to make your pack and leave. If you are here at that time, we will hang you from that tree."

Sam hustled. Before time was up, he was making tracks fast in the distance. He was never seen there again.

III: Into the Trinities

10. Traveling to the Trinity River

THE WINTER OF '50-'51 was somewhat strenuous outside, but on the whole agreeable in camp. We had a good house, plenty of provisions; Phillips was a good camp mate; Ben and I could get along with the others.

In the spring there was a change. Phillips left and said he was going home. I doubted it. He did not like his partner, whom he had known at home. But he left.

Ben had letters from home: His widowed sister had married, so she and the child had left the homestead. She urged Ben to come home. He thought he could buy out the heirs and, with his mother and a possible wife, have rest and peace. In the summer he went home.

I took as partners two men from Massachusetts and New Hampshire: J.A. Rich from Massachusetts and Pierce from New Hampshire; good fellows, good workers, good habits, and good men to join blankets with, especially Jerry who took the place of Ben as my friend. We were partners while I remained in the country. We had no strikes, but made some more than expenses.

In the autumn we were surprised at the return of Phillips, with his brother who had come out and joined him at San Francisco; they had not seen one another in twelve years. There had been a rush to Gold Bluffs, near the mouth of the Klamath. This was a rocky shore on the Pacific, which by the wear of the ocean had left gold deposits available at low tide. Phillips and his brother had gone there by sea. They were not successful, had drifted to Trinity River, a branch of the Klamath, which flowed westward equal in volume to the Sacramento or San Joaquin, but no harbor at its mouth; rapid, rocky and not navigable to any great extent. A great salmon river. They had found deposits on the Trinity of, as Phillips thought, an unlimited extent that could be wrought by sluicing with a large party.

The drawback was the hostile Indians. The Indians of the San Joaquin and lower Sacramento lived on the sparse productions of the earth, never cultivating the ground; they were not skillful hunters, but had bows and arrows skillfully made; they had but little clothing and were covered with lice. They would come around, looking so miserable and starved that we would give them old clothes and food.

"*Pokeeto, Gyata Wallah,*" they would ask, "a little food, friend."

Of course, it was not in human nature to refuse. The next day we would have more of them, and soon the whole tribe, leaving vermin invariably, and it was a constant warfare we had to get rid of them and to boil our clothes at least once a week. I had a camp mate who was careless of conditions; an old sailor. I said to him, "Bob, are you not lousy?"

"No, I never had a louse in my life." He was inclined to be angry at the suggestion.

I brought him a comb. "Let me see you comb your head." Somewhat reluctantly he did so and brought out a comb full.

"Holy Mackerel, Bob! You think it a disgrace to be lousy. Everybody is. I am. The governor of California is. Now use that comb and boil your clothing."

I have seen in the Sacramento Valley in hot weather a whole tribe basking in the sun, not a shred of clothing on any of them. Having no property, living on the spontaneous productions of the earth, they would steal and commit outrages.

I must pay a tribute to the Spanish in their treatment of the Indians. The government made grants to the pioneers of vast tracts of land. Captain Sutter, a Swiss soldier of fortune, had a grant of sixty square leagues where the city of Sacramento is now, then called Sutter's Fort. When I was there it was standing, an adobe building with tile roof. In the specifications of the grant was the civilization and Christianizing of the Indians and the organization of the missions of the Roman Church; their orders of celibates were adapted to the case. The Indians were rounded up, taught through ceremonies the elements of Christianity, morals, decency, agriculture, and so on. We would meet an Indian superior in mein and say, "That is a mission Indian." Wherever the Spanish rule extended, the Indian was not exterminated but cultivated to a certain extent. Witness the half-caste Republics of Mexico, Central and South America where they are slowly working out their salvation

III: Into the Trinities

through tears and blood, the universal rule of life. The Indians of the upper Sacramento and Klamath were of a different type.

❦

WE WERE SURPRISED BY the return of Ben within three months of his departure. He was ashore but twenty days.

"What is this?" I asked.

"Home is no place for me. Charles [his bachelor brother] has got everything into his hands without cost to him and I have no place." (His brother was a confirmed bachelor, a hard man.)

I found it was a chapter of disappointments. When Ben had arrived in New Milford unannounced, the up and down trains pass each other there. As he came out, he met a wedding party taking the other train. It was the girl "who might have been" to him. I understood, though he never said so, that life was never worth living to him afterwards. The ripple had closed, caused by us in the stream of time, and waters flowed smoothly.

Ben was welcomed by us heartily. He joined in with Phillips and me, and we prepared for the four hundred mile trip to the Trinity, and to us, "If the path is dangerous known, the danger's self is lure alone."[23]

We bought three burros, in Spanish pronounced "booroo," with the accent soft and lisping on "oo" as in *boost*. What a damnable word the American language had made it, spelling and pronouncing it "burro." The Klamath Indians would not eat them; horses and mules they would. Our New England friends made a party for us the night before we left. They were good fellows, and we had a high old time. We cached our tools in the log house, which we gave to the Frenchman and

---

[23] From *The Lady of the Lake* by Sir Walter Scott:
"A warrior thou, and ask me why!
Moves our free course by such fixed cause,
As gives the poor mechanic laws"
Enough, I sought to drive away
The lazy hours of peaceful day;
Slight cause will then suffice to guide
A knight's free footsteps far and wide,
A falcon flown, a gray-hound strayed,
The merry glance of mountain maid;
Or, if a path be dangerous known,
The danger's self is lure alone"

49

his Mexican wife, the brave little woman who had the blood of Castile and Montezuma in her veins.

Phillips was in charge of the pack animals. Packing with the "diamond hitch" was one of the fine arts. The rest of us roamed free, all there for the unpack at night. There was a friend from home at Sonora, some twenty miles away, we expected. He did not come, so I said I would wait for him another day and would come on and overtake them. So I stayed with our friends. He did not come, so as soon as it began to grow light, I said, "Good bye," and started. The first ten miles was "down a darksome glen"[24] until it came to the Stockton and Sacramento road. I had found the light was moonrise. Where I came out to the road, there was a "wayside inn." They had the biggest dog I ever saw. He was loose, the color of a Holstein bull and, as he came for me in the darkness with the voice of one, he loomed up as large.

I raised my gun and shouted, "Get out!"

He stopped and I got out. If I shot, the result would have been serious to the dog and to me likewise, if the owners could overtake me. I made twenty-six miles. At sunrise I stopped and got breakfast, and then went on. Soon I overtook the party. They didn't see me so I went around a hill, came in ahead, without looking back. I went on awhile, turned, shouted as though not knowing them, "Have you seen a party bound north?"

We kept on with them, Jerry and I together. We came to a ranch between the Moquelemne and Cosumnes Rivers, an American and his wife, proprietors. A well-bred woman gave us dinner, a table set in civilized style, dinner cooked and served by our hands. I had not spoken to a civilized woman since I left San Francisco nearly three years before, and to talk to a lady was an experience. A well-appearing man from the city was with us at the table.

I asked him, "How far is it to Winter's bar on the Moquelemne?"

"Twenty miles."

---

[24] From *The Lady of the Lake* by Sir Walter Scott:
The wily quarry shunned the shock,
And turned him from the opposing rock;
Then, dashing down a darksome glen,
Soon lost to hound and Hunter's ken,
In the deep Trosachs' wildest nook
His solitary refuge took.

III: Into the Trinities

I said, "Then I have walked twenty miles today."

I saw he did not believe me. Continuing the conversation he spoke of a large nugget of gold being found at a given place lately. There had been found sometime before some ten miles from us the largest nugget of gold ever heard of. I told of the find. (It was not very healthy to intimate that the teller of stories was a liar.) We will listen to an incredible story with seeming interest as one accustomed to miracles and tell one to match it. The stranger then told a story I knew was a lie.

Jerry said after we left, "That man thinks you are the greatest liar in California."

When we had come into camp, I had put sixty miles between us. We came to Sacramento or Sutter's Fort, bought supplies for our destination—a small blacksmith's bellows, a pitsaw to saw lumber, some carpenters tools—and packed the burros to the limit.

※

IN SACRAMENTO, THE SALMON season was on, and it was served at the eating houses. Fresh salmon is a revelation on fish. We saw the gill nets and seine traps used in Sacramento. Phillips said the Klamath and tributaries were full of them. He could knit nets, and we could go into the business profitably. We could get all we wanted to eat, anyway. So we got twine accordingly.

Our journey was on the west side of Sacramento which, with the valley of San Joaquin, is not available for irrigation, the streams from the coast range being denuded in summer. There torrents of winter left dry beds. It was a great cattle range: vegetation of the annual type, no turf, but starting with the autumnal rain matured in the spring and ripening as the dry season came on, retained its nutriment. Not being bleached by rain or dew, and with its seeds, it was very nutritious. The wild oats flourished and were practically the only vegetation for a great extent of country; an ideal forage for pasture or hay. Wheat, oats, and barley could be raised without irrigation. They were beginning to be cultivated. We sought a field of barley, some one hundred acres. The tallest of our party going into it could not see out. There was a beaten road we traveled, with wayside houses all deserted since the stage line on the east side of the valley was established.

Crossing at Coluso, some one hundred miles above Sacramento, we sometimes met a hunter at the old camps, which were surrounded by the bones and antlers of the elk, antelope, jack-rabbits (a species of hare), and sometimes the bones of the grizzly bear. There were teams of light drivers, collectors of the hunters' labors for the markets of San Francisco.

At night the yelp of the coyote, the mournful howls of gangs of large wolves, and the scream of the elk—a shrill, prolonged whistle—denoted we were not alone among living. The California deer is a mountain animal seldom seen on the plains, as was the mountain lion, a large panther.

11. Pests

I REMEMBER ONE NIGHT we came to a deserted house with the sign up "The Ohio House," with cook stove, stables, bunks in running order, so we essayed to use them accordingly. But we beat a retreat. The fleas covered us, active and hungry. My good neighbor, the late Colonel Hine, was talking to me one day, when he sat down hastily, removed his shoe and stocking, turned and examined it closely, then whipped it across the fence.

"What's the matter, Colonel?"

"There is a flea somewhere here."

"One flea," I laughed. "You ought to be in California where you would have ten thousand legion on you."

"Well, I don't want gold at that price."

The flea has a somewhat fastidious nature. Some he will bite, some he will not. Those he will, he will camp on and will skip, jump, prance, and crawl, and make life not worth living. The ones he bites suffer less, I think. They would not bite me, but I was their favorite camping ground. My old friend, Captain Whitmore of Massachusetts, financed several young men, our personal friends. One morning as I passed his camp, I saw him with his shirt off and, his countenance expressing anger and earnestness, he was whipping a tree with it.

"What's the matter Captain?"

"Oh, these cussed fleas. I don't care about their biting but this damned treading about I can't stand."

There was a small gnat the size of a pinhead but an efficient biter.

III: Into the Trinities

And the mosquitoes: A man from Oregon, working down the Sacramento in a boat with wife and children, said he had to keep a fire on the bow to make way by burning their wings off. On the Calaveras River wrapped in my blanket, I would fancy their bills in hypodermic suction, penetrating through blankets and clothes in search of blood.

The yellow hornet is similar in habitat to the smaller ones here that make nests in the ground of our meadows, but larger and more numerous; the Indians hunt for them and eat the larvae in their cones. Those hornets are in your food and clothes. Meat eaters. A piece of beef hung up of ten pounds would be carried off in two or three days. Their shear-like jaws would cut a piece out as large as a pea. A Mexican friend with his boys near us dressed as usual with the shirt outside pants. One got under his back and being cramped, made demonstrations. His antics and yells for his boys to get it out set us into convulsions. When order was restored in a serious way, he said, "*Mucho malo, hombre*" [very bad to laugh at him].

The tarantula, a large spider with spread of legs about three inches, is black with short hairs on body and the legs. I would tease them with a stick. They would fight and had fangs like a poison snake. They are poisonous in a hot climate.

The centipede, said to be poison, about three inches long of a dull green color, is very active. I would chop them in pieces with my shovel, and every piece would crawl.

The scorpions: I saw them only in Trinity River. The pictures of them in the old almanacs are true to life. They were among the small stones beside the river. One of my camp mates was stung on the thigh as he lay on the ground. He was in agony from it, and there was a purple spot the size of a hand. He stripped and lay in the cold water and mud of the river, and after a time was relieved of the pain and had no bad result afterwards.

The flies were negligible. I have seen them in the Sacramento Valley in their household duties. Men with flies crawling over their faces, seemingly unconscious of their presence. Such is habit.

∞

REPTILES: THERE WAS LIZARD about four to six inches long. A funny fellow. Quick as a flash, fearless, would run over the ground, your personal flycatcher. I was dressing one day. One ran up my back, resting on my shoulder. I yelled to Ben, not knowing what it was, "Get that off!" Ben shouted with laughter. I was angry with him. The cold feet on my back made it an unpleasant sensation. I would let them run on my hands. Hold them within six inches of a fly, they would jump and catch it every time. Their running feet on the dry ground would make the buzz-saw sound of the rattlesnake, the most nerve-cutting sound on earth.

Once on Trinity River I was walking hastily and stepped in a bunch of scrub grape vines, and heard the sound; I paid not much attention, thinking it was a lizard; I heard it again. I went back. The largest rattlesnake I ever killed lay coiled there. I must have stepped square on it.

The rattlesnake stands at the head of California snakes. The upper Sacramento and Trinity Rivers were infested with them, more than the San Joaquin and tributaries, though they were in evidence there. There are others. There were two moccasin snakes, the upland and water; the latter, the cottonmouth of the southern states, I was more afraid of them than the rattlesnake. A quick, active snake. Happening to go to my blankets one day on the Trinity, I found one coiled up about five feet long, snug and warm. For some time afterwards I shook the blankets before I went into them in the darkness. I knew a man who was bitten by a rattlesnake in his blankets.

There was a striped snake, in appearance to those here [in New England]. They were poison, I think, as they would show fight. They were tree climbers. Passing under an old oak once, some mice came down before me, and looking up, I saw one of these snakes, about a foot of which was swaying out of a hollow limb. I shot it.

The rattlesnake goes into business young, when he is more active and dangerous. The old snakes are clumsy, and will when striking reach some two-thirds of their length. Daggett, Ben, and I went on a tramp one day. A small snake crossed the trail. Ben was about to stamp on it.

"Hold on," said Daggett, "that's a rattlesnake."

Ben thought him joking and didn't stop. Daggett caught him and threw him aside, and killed the snake. It was young and frisky, a button on its tail, the bite as deadly as at any time of life.

A SIDE NOTE: The effect of animal poisons. Many years ago I read in the "Living Age"[25] an article on the effect and the remedy. The blood carries the poison and produces paralysis of the heart. The remedy is a powerful stimulant. The most powerful and quick-acting is spirits of ammonia, next spirits of camphor, ardent spirits, whiskey, brandy. I have known some bites of rattlesnakes cured by whiskey, not as counteracting the poison, but in keeping up the action of the heart.

The Journey to Shasta

JERRY AND I CARRIED SHOTGUNS. Sometimes we would kill quail, which has habits and size about the same as here; color and voice are different. Once at nightfall a flock arose and came down near a bush. It was near dark. I could see a dark bush. I shot at it, and went and got six, so we had broiled quail for supper.

We would amuse ourselves by blowing the snakes to pieces as we found them. There were plenty of them.

In one episode, Jerry and I started one morning before the rest. The sun was blazing hot; we walked some ten or twelve miles and no water; we had reached the limit of endurance. We came to a drove of cattle with a Missourian in charge. He had brought them across the plains and mountains.

"Have you any water?"

In his Pike County drawl, he said he had some "in a pail"—opaque with mud and mosquito larvae. We essayed to drink some and moisten our mouths with mumbles and curses. "Wa'al now, I allow the water is bad. I have some milk. I can make you some milk punch."

"Christopher Jerusalem! Make some. Don't put too much whiskey in it. We shall drink some."

He made it. We found it met conditions, and we drank until the drought was quenched. We started out, the sun hotter than ever experienced, the perspiration exhaling from us like the escape pipe of a steam engine. The whiskey in the punch took effect. We were making good time and going it. There was a rattlesnake crossing the trail. I fired without aim in my haste; did not hit it, caught a lose bush near, hit it

---

[25] "Living Age" was a weekly literary periodical, published from Boston, 1844-1941. Available online from the U.S. Library of Congress at
http://memory.loc.gov/ammem/ndlpcoop/moahtml/title/livn.html.

one crack and, with my low-cut hobnail walking shoes, jumped on it and stamped it and ground it into a fleshy mass that did not squirm. Jerry could tell a good story, and if he had materials he could make one, so by the campfire that night, he pictured the scene to the entertainment of the crew.

"Well, Jerry, you have done justice to the case except you have left yourself out. I don't doubt your seeing snakes. You were not shooting or stamping on any."

Trekking to the Trinity Mountains

THERE WERE NONE OF the party habitual drinkers. I had enough of that the first summer, but in the intercourse of all sorts and conditions of men, I have experienced most of the conditions that men meet in ordinary life, and when one tells an experience, I say, "I know, I have been there."

We continued together something more than a year after the forgoing incident, and I never drank intoxicating liquors and never saw any of our party do it. We came to the Sacramento at Colusa, some one hundred mile above Sacramento. A white cone broke the horizon line of the plain. It was Mount Shasta, something over a hundred miles away. The country was better watered, more elevated, but the plain continued.

We came to a public house, a hunters' camp. We had seen bear tracks on the trail, indicating enormous animals. The hunters had caught a cub that morning, and had him tied up, a fierce smiling chap. We encountered no old ones. They said, "If you come across one, offer him peace. They are hard to kill and dangerous. Get up a tree if you can, they cannot climb."

There were some dark spots in the distance on the plain. They were elk. One night as we approached the head of the valley, we camped some ten miles from Shasta village, the head of wagon transportation. Some muleteers camped near us. It rained that night and was intensely dark. In the morning we saw them standing around unusually. I went to them and said, "What's up?"

They said that the Indians had stolen their blankets, having crept upon them, jerked them off, and escaped in the darkness. Afterwards, a man told me of his experience near there with a party.

III: Into the Trinities

They had heard a noise. "One of the party rose up. He was immediately filled with arrows and was killed. I lay low as did the others and was uninjured."

☙

SHASTA IS NEAR THE western divide from the Klamath in the foothills, thirty miles from our destination. It's somewhat over twenty miles to the top of Trinity Mountain to the divide, seven miles from the summit down to the river. There's a grand panorama from the mountain top: eastward the valley of the Sacramento; the Sierra Nevada in the distance in the northwest; Mount Shasta, over fourteen thousand feet; coast range forming the horizon line, the mountain tops covered with snow, showing stunted trees some two weeks later than in the valley. The trail is impassable in the winter.

12. Placer Mining in the Trinities

THE MOST NOTABLE THING we saw descending the mountain in the deep canyons were the tall trees, seeking sunlight and defended from winds, trees twenty inches in diameter and two hundred feet high, as straight as arrows; firs and pines. I spoke of them to D.B. Mooney, proprietor of the ferry.

"You have never been down to Humboldt?"

"No," said I.

"Well, there's timber there. These are huckleberry bushes. I saw one thirty-three feet in diameter, three hundred feet before you come to a limb, knot, or hole."

We went on and camped at our destination and assumed possession according to miners' usage. I had doubts of Phillips' sagacity for the first time. On prospecting, there was gold there, but the amount in proportion to the earth to be handled and the waster obtainable at the height required did not strike me as remunerative, but we laid our plans to work.

☙

PLACER GOLD MINING HAS many phases or degrees; some I have worked out; but the final end of scientific action was done after I left the country. The first is the shovel, pick and pan in the small gulches, with a shallow depth of earth. We would prospect, digging to the bedrock, take a pan to the nearest water, and remove the earth and find the gold, if any, from the color; that is, a fine particle of paying quantity. Mexicans seldom use anything else but a wooden bowl, carrying it on their heads.

Earth that would not pay in that way would pay with a cradle rocker, which some five or six feet long, with a box at the upper end and a sheet-iron bottom perforated with holes half an inch in diameter. The earth was shoveled into the receptacle and water added simultaneously; the earth washed away, and the gold and weighty material would be obtained in the riffles at the bottom of the rocker. The box at the top was then taken off, the stones poured out, and the process repeated.

Then there was the "Long Tom" on the lesser grade of earth. It's a flat bottomed trough or sluice some twenty inches wide, twelve feet long. When the sluice was set at the proper height, the upper end would be at a rise of one feet in six. Two or three men could shovel in, and one man would tend the plate, stirring and shoveling out stones as the earth washed through the plate to a box underneath, a competent stream of water coming in at the upper end.

The "Long Sluice" was the plan we were to work with; this was the "Long Tom" made longer by adding lengths with sections as long as could be shoveled into, keeping in mind about three feet rise to about twelve feet length. Therefore, to use a sluice, there must be an ample supply of water at a proper height. There was no water to be had except from the river, by which the deposit was made, the bar being formed by the erosion and deposit of the river.

In the primeval days when the water sought the ocean by gravity, the tendency was straight ahead. Coming upon an obstruction, the earth was worn away by the force of the current, depositing the erosion on the opposite side below, as commonly seen on all streams. The primitive erosion on such streams as the wild-flowing Trinity, which almost flows white, leaves the bars higher than the present river bed. The difficulty of raising the sluices is apparent.

৪০

III: Into the Trinities

THE WATER WHEN WE came there was at its height, so that it looked as though we could cut a ditch some ways up the stream and carry water on the bar. So we made a division of labor.

My province was sawing out boards for sluices. I had seen saw pits in use in New York shipyards, one man above and one below, apparently simple in action. Of course, we had not teams to move logs, so I selected the base of a hill (we were in a deep, narrow valley) and made a platform of the proper height. We had no crosscut saw. Everything was done with the axe. With Pierce of New Hampshire, a giant in strength, we essayed to saw.

In the meantime, we were convinced of the necessity of a house. A few nights after we entered on our premises, we lay on the ground as usual, no shelter, our tools and grub, the camp kettles and equipage near, my gun standing against a tree at my head, the others likewise. We were sleeping the sleep of tired men.

In the morning everything was conspicuous by its absence. The Indians had cleared the camp and not a sound disturbed us. They were probably twenty or thirty miles away in the trackless mountains. There was nothing to do but for Phillips to take the burros and go over the mountains to Shasta for supplies.

Some, under the direction of Ben and Jerry were to make a house. There were plenty of pine trees on the bar, some two hundred feet high, pretty large to handle, but they cut and log-rolled and made an Indian-proof house. The prospects were so discouraging that two of the party left for the south.

Those Indians kept everything under surveillance. We would hear a coyote calling in the woods or on the mountain, or a large owl, and the answered call at a distant point; perfect in imitation. We knew it was the Indians. They knew the number in every party. If we were out of sight, they would swoop down, steal and vanish, stealing the camp kettle off the fire.

There were some mule packers camped down the river some distance. They watched their mules at night alternately. Those on watch went to camp a short distance away to change watch; those whose turn it was found no mules. At daylight they took the trail; a short distance away they found a dead mule, one ham cut out. They followed the trail some one hundred miles but never saw an Indian or a mule.

℘

59

AS THE WATER LOWERED in the river in consequence of the snow disappearing from the mountains, we saw we could not ditch it to the sluice, so we concluded to build an Egyptian waterwheel. This was to build a wheel similar to the wheel of a steamboat, anchor it in swift water with buckets on the rim which would fill as the wheel turned and empty into a box near the top, connected with a conductor to the sluice. So we cut two large logs, rolled them into the river, anchored them as near level as we could as a foundation the proper distance apart; on them we built our wheel.

Jerry was a builder, having built railroad bridges. I sawed the lumber, the hardest labor of my life. The pit sawyers must work with the most exact rhythm. They are out of sight of each other. The top sawyer—my place—must give the motion, direction and feed, and the bottom sawyer must take the rhythm and feed from him. Before we got it, I thought it would kill me, but it must be done and it was. The wheel was built and successfully operated. We could raise the water within two feet of the diameter of the wheel. Of course, the water must be kept in the turning stream at a uniform depth and velocity. With infinite labor, we did that. The wheel turned constantly, night and day, creaking and groaning.

Phillips made a gill net for catching salmon, which we anchored across the river, the water being the clearest I ever saw, coming from the snowy mountains, not being turbid from the working of the diggings as was the Sacramento, San Joaquin and tributaries. The salmon would come to the gill net, in their fool obstinacy refuse to stick their heads into it, would give a leap over it, and so on they went. We never caught one.

The people along the river were from the South and West. We were the only New Englanders. This was before the East was connected with the West and South by railroad, and the manners and customs of the sections were not as cosmopolitan as at present. I could generally tell where a man came from by his dress, actions, speech, and manner. We Yankees were looked down upon until we commanded respect by doing things, and we would neither do nor suffer injustice, and we made friends.

Mooney's Ferry

DENNIS B. MOONEY, PROPRIETOR of the ferry, from Mississippi, was one of the most remarkable men I ever met. I would like to give a character sketch of him, but I have no space for it here. Through him and others, I knew something of southern and frontier life. He was a pioneer pathfinder, conducted one of the first wagon-trains across the plains and mountains, one of the first on the Trinity. He spoke of his friend, General Denver[26], who was then in California; many years afterwards he was the pioneer in Colorado gold-diggings.

Mooney had two ferries on the Trinity, one some thirty miles above us. He said General Denver had obtained a charter for him for a highway from Shasta over the Divide to cross the ferry where we were to the county seat, some twelve miles below Weaverville. About a mile above, some others had built a bridge so that animals could cross, and this took business from him. He had the exclusive right by charter to construct a road for wheels with bridge to operate the same, but had not been able to capitalize it so far, but did so afterwards and made it remunerative.

Mooney was popular and deserved it. His roadhouse at the ferry was a gathering place for the public. It was the entertainment of our lives to attend political meetings there, when a squad of candidates on horseback came from distant parts of opposing interests and parties. Candidates from county judge and county sheriff, down to justice of the peace addressed the voters with characteristic manners and oratory. We used to read about it in papers as specimens of the western oratory, and supposed none was never equaled by the addresses we heard at Mooney's roadhouse.

One of the best speakers was a candidate for county judge. He was a lawyer, a capable man seemingly, who had killed his man in an affray on the frontier and left his state for the good of it. He was opposed by one of similar type, and their speeches were entertaining in personalities. He was defeated. It was an awful place for the unscrupulous and inefficient. They both went down. The last I heard of him, he had stolen

---

[26] General James William Denver, who served in the California state government and U.S. House of Representatives, U.S. Commissioner of Indian Affairs, and governor of the Kansas Territory.

from a fellow-passenger a bag of gold on the Sacramento stage. He was detected and was in the chain-gang at Sacramento.

The Ferry Pier "Bee"

THE SELF-ACTING FERRIES WERE new to me. A cable rope was stretched across the river and fastened securely, with a pulley block running on the rope on each end, the forward end near the cable, the rear further off, so as to be diagonal to the stream; the force of which would propel it across; then, by loosening the fore and tightening the rear, the return was made. Mooney was building a bridge, and had made the piers at ends and one at the middle—cribs made of logs, filled with stones, spaces some sixty feet between. He had sleepers hewed of heavy timbers to place on them. So he had a "bee," inviting all in the vicinity, our party included. We being the only Yankees, strangers to the others, would show our efficiency, which we did to their somewhat envious surprise. There were many young fellows I mated with[27] in their somewhat rough sports on the ferry-boat and on the river.

Someone said, "I should like to see someone get in here today."

Thinks I to myself, "I think he will."

So in a crowded boat and seeing a favorable opportunity, I pushed him in. I was astonished of course, and he thought it was someone else. They were mostly good swimmers. He got on the boat, and of course the one he thought pushed him went in also. The water was icy cold, some twelve feet deep, the current swift. It used to be said it was fatal to get into it.

I shouted to their best swimmer, a fellow of my own age and caliber, "Help, here!" and plunged in; he did also and we both gasped, him almost simultaneously.

Sternly I said, "Keep quiet," as though I should duck him if he did not, as I probably should. He obeyed and I swam ashore with him. They saw I was at home and efficient, and we mated. Mooney gave us good dinner and we had a high time. They told stories of western life and across the plains, which I matched with sea yarns. One sample of theirs

---

[27] Buckingham uses the phrase "mated with" following the now rare usage defined in the Oxford English Dictionary: "4. a. intr. To associate or keep company with. Now rare. ...1881 W. BESANT & J. RICE Chaplain of Fleet I. vii. 160 It was a shame that a gentleman of his rank should mate with men whose proper place was among the thieves of Turnmill Street."

was: A Dutchman and wife with team was making the journey. They came to a spring, so made their camp for the night and unharnessed. She took her tea-kettle to the spring to fill it and scalded her hand. It was a hot one. She ran for her husband.

"Hans, Hans, get up your teams and start. Hell is not a half mile off."

Sluicing Progress

WE HAD RAISED THE water and operated the sluice, but we were not getting all the gold. The force necessary to carry the water through took gold also, in spite of the riffles. The process of gold mining where the percentage of gold to earth was small was scientifically solved by hydraulic science and capitalization. Iron pipes were laid from distant points to get pressure; the stream, with great force directed against the bank, washed away the debris into the rivers and plains.

The "slickens," so called, were a great damage to agricultural lands, requiring legislation to regulate the case. Then what remained was washed through quicksilver machines, which would catch the gold for which it had an affinity, and the heavy sand and gravel would be discharged. This amalgam of gold and quicksilver would be strained through tanned deerskins, removing most of the quicksilver. The residue was put into a retort, by heat evaporated and condensed by water, and used indefinitely. The care of the wheel and the difficulty of adjusting the propelling stream was too much. With the winter flood, creaking and screaming with accelerating force, the whole business left its anchorage and went down river.

Ben, discouraged and restless, left for the southern mines. Pierce, the sturdy giant, not very intellectual but one of the best-hearted fellows in the world, had a brother whom he was working to educate. He heard of his illness and death, and left for home.

So the Phillips brothers, Jerry and I, remained of the party.

13. Life in Trinity County

ONE DAY A MAN rode into camp, dismounted, and said, "Gentlemen, I am the tax collector of Trinity County. I am here to receive your taxes."

I looked at him. I knew the type: the county officer, the gambler, and the thief, synonyms in California. It was universally known that no one sought an office there but as a license to steal. Of course, he had a revolver slung to his hip. I spoke for the company.

"Of course you can collect, as we have visible property, our tools, and sluices. I have paid taxes," said I, "since I came into the country but they never went there legitimately, and I don't suppose these will."

He was angry, but I think he saw we were not a good crew to have a row with, and on receiving the tax, he left. Afterwards, we heard when his collections were finished, he left and was left to human kin in the oblivion of the multitude.

Phillips was a crack shot and a hunter. There was a game bird, a grouse as large as a barnyard fowl. They were good eating. In all companies I was, in the office of steward and chef was conceded to me. He would go out and get a grouse when needed, and my game stews were celebrated.

One day he was down the river about a mile in the hills from the roadhouse, where mule trains rested and unpacked. He heard an unusual noise, as of animals running. He stepped behind a tree and looked in the direction a drove of mules were coming and two Indians hurrying them up, armed with bows and arrows. As they came up, unconscious of his presence, he covered the big Indian with his gun and stepped out between him and the mules.

"Halt!"

The smaller fingered his bow and arrows, but the big Indian spoke to him, restraining action. Phillip motioned to him to head the mules and bring them back, which was done by the smaller one. He was looking the big Indian in the eye, and at the least sign was sure of him. The mules were headed back on the trail. He motioned them to follow. They refused, motioning that they had far to go to sleep before night. Phillips motioned them to go. His gun was a single barrel, and he could get but one; the other had a bow and arrows. They went. He watched them in the distance, then drove the mules to the road house, where their owners had left them for a few minutes preparatory to watching

III: Into the Trinities

them for the night. That was the only time any of us saw an Indian on the Trinity.

※

OVER THE DIVIDE OF the Trinity to the north is Scott's River, also a tributary of the Klamath, its valley with a great width of arable land. A colony from Missouri with families and cattle had located there. When the snow came, they were shut in with no supplies except their cattle. A limited supply of salt sold for one dollar an ounce.

They saw that the cattle would be insufficient to carry them through, so to reduce the number to feed, thirty men forced their way over to the Trinity, leaving some men behind with the women and children. As they came up the divide, they found the snow thirty feet deep. One would force his way until exhausted, then step to one side and go to sleep; the next would take his place, and the last in the line awake him; and so on until the summit was reached, when it turned to rain and they knew the snow would not be deeper. They all lay down and slept.

They came down on the Trinity like hungry wolves. They would come to a miner's house, camp, and would not be denied, and they would eat everything he had. We were on the other side of the river, which was impassable, and they were the worst set of men I ever saw. What clothes they had were rags drenched with wet. They scattered themselves along the river in the mining camps, and we expected to hear that their comrades with the women and children were all starved. But we heard they were all saved by supplies forced through from Oregon.

The deer failed, leaving us to the beans. So we came through nine days, twenty-seven meals in succession. There were some Missourians below. As they came up, I said, "Well, boys, how did you get along?"

"Wa'al, right smart. We ate our jackass, and our dogs, and came through all right."

Finally, coming over the divide I saw some mules with sacks of flour on their backs. I went to them. "What do you ask for the flour?"

"We have not any to sell."

"What are you going to do with it?"

"We are going down to Weaverville. You will not pay what we can get for it there."

"How do you know? I want some flour."

"We'll let you have some, a few pounds for a dollar and a half a pound."

"Well, if you can get over, I think we can. We have some beans left."

I never tasted anything as good as the bread we got from that flour.

❧

PHILLIPS STARTED WITH THE burros. He managed to get through and brought news from the outside. The Sacramento River was thirty or forty miles wide. Thousands of horses and cattle drowned. River-craft navigable water over the plains brought relief from below. Sacramento city flooded to the second story of the buildings.

We made a canoe-shaped boat to get over the river, where we found diggings that weren't rich, but we could make our grub. The waves in the river ran four feet high in the center, so we would kneel in the bottom and work our way up with shovels as paddles. We would strike in, keeping our bow upstream so as to be diagonal to the current and the waves, and then we'd paddle for dear life on the lower side, going down a quarter of a mile or so to the other side. So we worked a few days, out of sight of the house.

On returning at noon one day, I saw the door open and said, "Boys, the Indians have been down on us."

We got over and found it so. We were cleaned out. Nothing was left but the shirt, pants, and boots we stood in. Our blacksmith bellows were cut open to find the contents.

We hurried up the river, borrowed rifles, struck the trail, and followed it until night fall, but it was of no use, for they could make tracks or leave signs faster than we could find them. The only vestige we found was a trunk valise I had, with specimens of gold, souvenirs of South American cities and of California, foreign coins, my letters, and other things of value to me. Jerry had a watch with a hunting case. They had opened the valise, taken out the watch, set it one edge, and cracked it open as a nut to get the contents, the works, and then left the case as of no value. We returned, of course, carrying the rifles back to the owners.

III: Into the Trinities

14. Dennis B. Mooney and the Stockton Road

IN THE LAST [CHAPTER], we had returned from the Indian trail, and as trailing is a science as certain as any other, I speak of that and illustrate by incidents.

I returned south. A Mexican near us had saddle mules. He rented one to my camp mate for a trip of some thirty miles. Ten miles down "the darksome glen"[28] to the Calaveras and the Stockton Road, there was an almost constant passing of pack animals and freight wagons. My camp mate went on that road ten miles, where a track of a single animal would be obliterated in a few minutes, and then left the road, back to camp—ten miles or more.

Two or three days afterwards, the mule strayed and the Mexican sent his Indian boy to find it. He took a circuit round the camp until he struck the track made by my camp mate. The boy, not knowing of the use of the mule by my camp mate, followed it down the glen to the Stockton Road, thence the ten miles where there were footprints up to the turn for camp; the boy came in, sure of his trail. He was right as to the trail, but it was an old one. The mule had returned during his absence.

This would seem uncanny. The explanation is simple. Every animal in nature has its footprint. Probably nothing in nature has its exact duplicate. The multitude of mankind has not the same finger marks. The burros that we had had footprints as distinct as fingerprints, and these are today still in my memory, as are the animals. The Indian knew the footprints of every one of his master's mules. He followed the tracks to the Stockton road, then took one side of the road and found no footprints, then the other and found none, back and forth, so on until he struck the footprint where he turned off and returned to camp. At night he lay down and slept. He was gone two days. This is the science acting on comprehensible facts.

In our case, where we traced the Indians, there wasn't a footprint. We circulated round the house-camp until we came to the untrod wilderness. Nature has acted in a certain degree of uniformity. The leaves,

---

[28] From Sir Walter Scott, "The Lady of the Lake":
 Then, dashing down a darksome glen,
 Soon lost to hound and hunter's ken,
 In the deep Trosach's wildest nook
 His solitary refuge took.

plants, the pebbles are so deposited or grown. We find a blade of grass turned out of the given order, a leaf turned over, a pebble displaced. We were on the trail. I could trail the Indians as he could trail me.

More About Dennis B. Mooney

IN A WAY, I AM telling of my schoolboy days and of the influence by which my character was formed; and of my teachers, among whom I count this man.

The next day after the episode of our being cleaned out, Mooney came down to us and said, "There is no business doing at my roadhouse and ferry at present. My caretaker in an old man who I am going to send to San Francisco to friends I have there. They will get a position as caretaker on a ship for him. I am going to stay at my upper ferry for a time. You will do me a favor if you will move up and occupy my house. There are provisions, blankets, cooking utensils, and so on. You can have the provisions at cost. The place is not as exposed as this, and the Indians will let you alone. What do you say?"

I said, "Holy God! What can we say? Are you an angel? Take off your shirt and let us see your wings."

Before and subsequently, in casual conversation, I got the story of my life from him. He was one of the most perfect men in physical form I ever saw, and he was as good as he looked. He was typical Southern gentleman, with the ideas of his environment. He was a slave dealer, as unconscious of wrong as I was, as he described his going north after Negroes (he was a native of Mississippi).

Mooney's life was instructive of conditions of environment. He spoke of his courtship. After a short interval of marriage, a lady's husband died, leaving her a large plantation. An attractive woman. He became interested, and according to custom, made advances in the usual way by asking if he might be permitted to attend church with her. She responded with permission, and the next Sunday he walked to church with her dressed in his best, carrying her book. He sat with her, joined in the devotions as a gentleman should; she, on the return, invited him to dine, and so on.

"I took a mental view," says he, "at the prospect. The responsibilities were too great. That immense property, the care of the Negroes and her welfare, I did not feel equal to, and we parted with regret, I think on both sides."

III: Into the Trinities

The subsequent life convinced me, as he told it, that he made a mistake. He was equal to any position he was ever in. He was captain of a pioneers' wagon train for California. I have been acquainted with several, and the responsibility and the universal genius is infinite of the explorer. One incident he related:

"We had come into a seemingly waterless country. I was on horseback, the train slowly following. I went up a mountain to get a prospect. In the distance (and you can see a great way there) was a mountain. I thought I could see a green spot there. Perhaps there was water. So I went for it. It took me almost all day. Blazing hot, I was parched with heat and starving with hunger. I came to a band of Indians who evidently had never seen a white man. I made them understand my thirst and hunger by signs. They brought me water, then food, dried grasshoppers or locusts. I couldn't get much down. Some dried seeds of plants, not much good in them. Some dried meat that was better. So recuperated, I started back for the train. It was nightfall when I found it, and the women and children were crying and screaming for water, and the men not much better. I hustled the train forward to the small spring, and it was a busy night watering the train and filling the water barrels."

He was a pioneer on the Trinity, had been on the mountain tops of the Divide, and thus knew the geography of the country and of the Indians. They said to him that he was the first white man they had ever seen. At first they were friendly, but that changed.

ଐ

A SIDE NOTE: I am informed that a, or the, Devil is an indispensable employee in a printing office, and as the origin of the species came from an Angel who became insubordinate to the law of Heaven, "where order is Heaven's first law,"[29] so the antithesis is the law of Satan's kingdom. The devils have stored energy which, being harnessed and educated, is made useful; but the inherent deviltry sometimes breaks out.

In my crowded memories in my articles I have sent to *The Bee*, in which I endeavor to keep within the bounds of reason and say as little as possible, I become garrulous at times, and no doubt try the patience of the devil himself as proofreader. I am made to leave out or misuse

---

[29] Alexander Pope, *An Essay On Man*, Epistle 1.

words essential to sense; so in my description in my communication in February, in the scene of the water scrap[30], some is left out. In pushing and scrambling in the water, one was pushed in who couldn't swim. I saw and shouted to one of the best swimmers to save the man, in peril of his life, and so on.

Other minor deviltry I pass over in the article. I make this explanation as my purpose is to do an exact justice, and the saying is, "give the devil his due." Give me my due also, so each shall work in harmony. As I have had many occasions in my life to work with the devil to accomplish desired results, and we have been good friends in so doing.

15. The Disputed Claim

THESE MEMORIES OF THOSE that I call my schoolboy days, my environmental and its educational effect, I find are much more than I anticipated when I commenced. In doing business over a telephone and meeting acquaintances, there is generally a remark, "I am so interested in the articles in the *Newtown Bee*. I hope you will continue them."

You remember I spoke of my aspirations which sent me to California and the bitter disappointment that resulted, but which might be expected on the lady's part; but not on mine, shut out of all society and dwelling on the past. How easy to end it all with a bullet through my head or drown it in dissipation and go into oblivion unwept and forgotten. But such a course would, on the part of the lady and her friends, justify their action in my rejection.

I said to her, "I should probably never be a fit mate for you, but I would not be despised. However humble my position and the dreary desert stretching before me, I would meet life as a man, and what ills I met I would conquer or bear."

I have shrunk from no encounter or head or hand and have not always been whipped. Some things can be done once, but should not be done twice. The readers of Lytton Bulwer's novels will remember the

---

[30] See "The Ferry Pier 'Bee'" topic in Chapter 12.

III: Into the Trinities

character Devereaux[31], a young soldier of fortune wishing to enter the service of the King of France, Louis XV. He had an encounter with the assailants of his king when Prince Philip of Orleans, incognito, was on a spree and rescued him in danger of his life; but he was not advanced. The king was in the habit, with the higher nobles of both sexes, to hold orgies, when all restraint was thrown off, so Devereaux managed to get there. The king was open to influence of wit or surprised at seeing him.

Said Devereaux, "I will tell you a story. A Jesuit on his rounds up and down the universe went to hell. Satan saw him and of course was preparing to initiate him with hellish rights. The Jesuit (the king did not like the order) pleaded for mercy, said he was a traveler seeing the country and had no designs of residence. (You know what a tongue the Jesuit has.) He convinced the good Satan of his innocent intentions, so he let him go. Finally the Jesuit died and of course went to hell. Satan saw him again and proceeded to action. The Jesuit pleaded as he had done before that he was only a traveler, and so on. No, says Satan, a traveler once, but the second time, the devil's for good."

❦

I HAD A REVEL FOR once, never repeated. It came about in this way: Ben and I had a camp mate "H" who had a father and brother that came after—not present when the instance I am speaking of happened. We did not like this camp mate, but we bore him without open offense. "H" had a difficulty with old Captain Whitmore and his "protegés" about a claim. Ben and I had struck them as reliable men, though we had not personal acquaintance. We passed, as people said when we became acquainted, "as orderly, inoffensive" (we always kept step and dressed alike in red shirts).

Whitmore's protegés offered to "H" to leave the case to the "red-shirted fellows" for arbitration. "H" agreed to abide by our decisions, believing that as camp mates we would decide in his favor. So, the case being stated to us, we with deliberation in private, gave our decision that "H" was wrong and he should pay a certain sum to the adverse party.

---

[31] Edward Bulwer-Lytton, *Devereux* (1829). The text can be found on Project Gutenberg at http://www.gutenberg.org/files/7630/7630-h/7630-h.htm.

Several days afterwards, "H" said that our decision was wrong and said, "I entered into their claim and Providence favored me, and I got gold enough to make it right."

I made no comment, but I saw the captain's boys and told them of "H's" theft. I said, "One of you come up this evening, and he shall pay you back."

So the man came up and stated the case to "H" (not saying where he got his information), and demanded restitution. "H" blustered and relapsed into bullying, and he declared he would not pay it. Then I took a hand.

"You blank liar and thief, you will pay that or hug a tree with a bare back. Ben and I have assisted in such cases, and we will in this. We have friends enough ready to help. Now be blank quick about it."

He was sulky but paid. His older brother and father soon after returned, and Phillips came from the north. We left the house and built another, and left them. We were about to depart for the North. "H" owed me for assisting him for working out a claim where water prevented one man working it.

I said to Phillips, "H is going away and has not paid me, and I am going down this evening to get it. There will probably be a row. I don't want you to fight my battles, but they respect you, and it may prevent a fight if you are there."

"All right" said he, "I'll go.

So we went and talked indifferently, until I said, "H, I hear you are going away, and I have come down for what you owe me."

He said, "You called me a liar and a thief the other day when I was sick, and I shan't pay you."

"Are you well now?"

"Yes."

"Then I repeat it." (There is a man in New Milford, an old soldier, Merritt Hunt, who was there.) Says I, "You are a bigger man than I. Now then, if you will go with me out on the plains, unarmed, alone, we'll balance accounts."

He did not accept.

I turned to "L," his brother, "What do you think of it."

"I think you must not call my brother a liar and thief in my presence."

Then old "R," a giant, struck in with language unfit to print. Phillips had said nothing before. He sprung to my side and shouted, "Blank, you come in. I won't see my friend and one I think so much of set upon in this way."

We were two to three, but they didn't come. We went home. The next morning "L," the older brother came to Phillips and attempted to smooth things over. Phillips said, "Don't talk to me; go to Ralph."

He came and said, "H shall pay you."

I said, "He probably will. If he don't by such a time today, I will go to Major Bornio, the Alcalde, with the debt and his record as a thief will be presented." He came up and offered me money at such a sum per day. I said "That will not settle it."

"I shan't pay any more."

I threw down my shovel, "Well, I'll see Major Bornio," and started off.

"Hold on, I will pay you." He did so and began to use disrespectful language. "

"Shut up your head, and take the trail you came on. If I hear another word from you, I'll whip you, or you will me. I hope I shall never see you again." He went, and I never saw him afterwards.

The day before we were to start for the north, the old captain sent one of the young men up, who said, "We want you and your friends to come down and have a parting bottle with us tonight."

I said to our chums, "We all know what that means. The jolly old soul, let us go give him something to remember us by." So at nightfall we went. I said, "You go on. I'll be there soon. I am going to see old R and L."

I went there and said, "Now we may never see one another again. I don't want any bad memories of you, and you don't want any of me. Let bygones be bygones." I offered my hand and they gave theirs.

"All right, we are glad you came. Let us drink to good fellowship." So they brought a tumbler about three-quarters full. I, supposing it to be half water and somewhat excited with emotion, said, "Here's hoping we may meet again in old Connecticut" and turned it down. I heard a note of astonishment.

"Heavens, was that clear whisky?"

"Yes, we have but one glass and poured out the drinks for three. We were going to let you drink first."

"Well, I'm in a nice fix. Captain Whitmore and his friends have invited us, down, and I am on my way there. I shall be as drunk as a boiled owl."

The Parting Bottle

THE CAPTAIN, JOLLY OLD soul, had a table full of brandy, whisky, and wine ready, and we went in. He said, "Charge your glasses. I will give you our friends the Buckinghams." This was done with cheers.

Ben says, "You respond."

"Well, gentlemen, I am neither an orator, poet, or singer, but like the immortal Bottom in *Midsummer Nights' Dream*, I can roar you like a lion, or anon, like the sucking dove.[32] In ancient times, it was the custom to make a ruler of the feast whose will must be obeyed. Now I think the captain is not a disinterested person. He is not stern enough to enforce order and sentence anyone to death for disobedience. I move that one of a more despotic disposition be appointed. What do you say?"

"Good," they shouted.

"I nominate the little Buckingham." The captain put it to vote, and it was carried with a yell.

"I accept the honor and lay down the law, which is like that of the Medes and Persians, binding on the king and his subjects alike, and which cannot be repealed by himself. Anyone who does not respond in full, or fails to drink when I hold up my glass to show the quantity or to sing a song, tell a story, or give a toast, shall take a bumper."

"What's that?"

"Four strong men shall take him, two at his arms and two at his legs, face upwards, and he shall be lifted up and down and bumped until he obeys."

"In honor of the captain, I will sing 'Hail to the Chief.' Ben, you remember when we and France Merwin were members of the New Milford Rifles with our blue uniforms with red trimmings and plumes. (By the way, you don't know Ben. We are the Siamese twins and grow together. He is as full of music as an egg is of meat. He could play on a snare drum with all intervening instruments to a keyed bugle You remember the night he was a Corporal of the Guard, and France was stationed on his beat before an old barn just over the line full of roughs

---

[32] William Shakespeare, *A Midsummer Night's Dream*: Act 1, Scene 2.

III: Into the Trinities

who were encroaching. France shouted, 'Corporal of the Guard.' I responded and went to the Captain of the guard from a company from another part of the county, who said, 'Take some of your blue devils and clean them out.' Of course, that was what I wanted, so I saw my captain and he gave me a delegation, Ben, France, and I in the lead and went through. The head rough didn't go through the door, but took three boards off when he went out. How France and I sung 'Hail to the Chief' with a roar that the immortal Bottom of *Midsummer Night's Dream* would have encored, and you gave the accompaniment on the bugle. Now, 'Hail to the Chief,' and when I swing my arm over my head at the chorus, it will be twice repeated. And if anyone fails to let himself out, you will know the penalty."

So there we were. I roared the song and they all roared the chorus. Now, I held my glass.

"Hold up your glasses. I give you that fine old noble gentleman, all of the olden time, Captain Whitmore. Long may he wave. Now can you all sing: 'A life on the Ocean Wave, a home on the Rolling Deep, where the raging waters rage and the winds their revels keep,'[33] and the chorus, 'O, give me the flashing brine and the spray and the tempest roar.' Jerry give us a story. You can. No excuses."

There was a Negro ball upstairs at the tavern, and tea was served to the ladies between the dances. Some devil put a paper of tobacco in the teapot. It was served. Soon the head of the ball appeared at the head of the stairs.

"Waiter. Here is a little hot water. The tea is a little strong for the ladies' stomach. Just right for the gentleman."

I have no space for the proceedings. The fun grew fast and furious. The old Captain lied.

"Here," says he, "you go up to Smith's and tell him Captain Whitmore wants so many bottles of brandy, and so many of wine. And I don't want any of his damned pizen stuff neither."

"Well, boys, all our sweethearts are sacred here. Captain, no doubt, has his. Perhaps like the Dutch gentleman, and old bachelor, his young friends probably thought he had none. Bump! What do you puppies

---

[33] "A Life on the Ocean Waves" was a popular song in New England in the 1850s; now the official song of the U.S. Merchant Marine Academy. See
http://en.wikipedia.org/wiki/A_Life_on_the_Ocean_Wave.

know? I have had two sweethearts at a time. Now, boys, we are all exiles from home and all things dear: a continent between us. I will give the 'Exile of Erin' and when the chorus comes, 'O Erin Mavoorneen. O Erin Go Bragh,'[34] roar as gentle as sucking doves."

At length I said, "The small hours are here. One of our party has retired and by his gentle breathing is sleeping the gentle sleep of childish innocence." (He was one who thought he could drink the rest down and said so, and we put him into his bunk long since, where he was snoring like the sound of a breaking sea on a rocky coast.) "Now, boys, we start on a four hundred mile tramp in the morning. Join hands all around and we sing. 'Shall auld acquaintance be forgot and never brought to mind.'"

I think there were wet cheeks when we parted. I walked home half a mile, went up a perpendicular pole with pegs, stepped to the side to the sleeping loft, as sober as any in that crew.

They told me in the morning that there were twenty-seven empty bottles. There were nine of us.

---

[34] Thomas Campbell, "Exile of Erin," (1777-1844). Last stanza:
Yet all its sad recollections suppressing,
One dying wish my lone bosom can draw:
Erin! an exile bequeaths thee his blessing!
Land of my forefathers! Erin go bragh!
Buried and cold, when my heart stills her motion,
Green by the fields, sweetest isle of the ocean!
And thy harp-striking bards sind aloud with devotion, -
Erin mavournin - Erin go bragh!
http://www.poetry-love-poems.com/campbell/exile-of-erin.php

☙

IV: Heading Back

16. Starting for Home

I HAVE WRITTEN HERETOFORE for "Society" spelled with a very small "s." I am about to change my environment to where it is spelled with capitals. Perhaps I should wait until the environment is changed, but the memories like the goblins in "Gabriel Grub"[35] are unruly.

These memories are not voluntary but are written by necessity and will continue whether published or not. I am an old man, eighty-six years of age, and sleep lightly. The demons of wakefulness torment me and stay their clamor. I light my lamp, and at my desk at the head of my bed I write, not knowing what will come next or what goblin will be uppermost. I was invariably the youngest of my partners. As a boy I was somewhat effeminate and, as my readers have probably seen, inclined to sentimentalize. I was inclined to inquire to the four "W's": What, Whence, Why, and Whither.

I went to a phrenologist when first in New York waiting for my ship to sail.

"Give my character in writing."

He did so. Nothing out of the common until he said, "You are very emotional, and you will do well to be on your guard in your loves and friendships."

How much he got from the shape of my head or from intuition and insight, from my own experience I am seldom wrong in my first glance at character.

Of the revel [hosted by Captain Whitmore]: I had taken charge and carried it through to the satisfaction of myself and others. There had been no obscenity or blasphemy. The old Captain's drinks were pure and left no bad effects, neither did the doings ethically. I kept correspondence with Jerry and some others many years. When, in after time,

---

[35] Charles Dickens, "The Story of the Goblins Who Stole a Sexton" in *The Pickwick Papers*.

the Honorable Jeremiah Rich, manufacturer and member of the Massachusetts Legislature, with the stationery of the Quincy House, Boston, wrote to me, among other things, "Do you remember the parting of friends at French Creek?"

The Physical Effects: I had drunk more intoxicants that night than any one of the party, and I think I was the least affected. The next day, as I have stated, was spent at my friends' camp, waiting for a companion who did not come. Then I started out to overtake the party and made my record for endurance, with sixty miles paced behind me that day. This was done by my general abstinence. A mistaken idea is that use is required to bear intoxicating drinks. From my observation, the contrary is a fact inevitable. The habitual drinker is the habitual drunk. With many of them, a single drink is in evidence. Examples crowd my memory. My health was perfect; not enfeebled by dissipation.

When I returned, I told my stories to my mother. I said to her, "Mother, I have told you everything. My hands are clean. I have not much money, but it is all mine. Not a dollar belongs to anyone but myself. My lips are as clean as you gave them to me. I have been through Hell, but there is no smell of brimstone about me."

With regards to the revel and the outlet of emotion: formerly, Christmas was the principal time. Scott says: "England was merrie when old Christmas brought its sports again. That only night in all the year saw the stolled priest the chalice rear."[36] John Phoenix somewhat tersely expresses his patriotism when he says, "A man who won't get drunk on the Fourth of July is a damned rascal."

Ethically: "There was a marriage at Cana of Galilee and Jesus and his mother were invited to the marriage [evidently poor people]. His mother said to him, 'They have no wine.' His reply was ambiguous. His mother said to the servants, 'Whatsoever he says to you, do it.' Some water pots were standing near. 'Fill the water pots with water. Draw out now and bear to the governor of the feast.'"[37]

Mark all the proceeding. The first and most important miracle Jesus ever performed. This was the place and time for emotion to be let loose, where men were supposed to get drunk. They had had some wine which was poor, and the governor had reproached the bridegroom for giving

---

[36] From *Marmion*, by Sir Walter Scott.

[37] John 2:3–5.

the poor wine before they were drunk enough to not distinguish it from good, and now the good wine was thus wasted and probably the best that ever was made. Emotions proper for occasions of marriage were thus enforced, the most solemn and important event in human life. The bringing together of two human beings in purity of body and spiritual communion to continue humanity and raise it in the scale of being. The mother church treats it as a sacrament, justly, and to be approached after confession and absolution, and the lighthouse of pain and death for the guide of humanity in the way of life, the terrible punishments for illegitimate intercourse, which wipe out individuals and nations and seem to prevent progress and high cultivation, and the advance of Society with a capital "S," with the inevitable decrease of the birth rate and the misplaced practice of destroying the bleeding sheep instead of the wolves who rent them. No words can express the wrath and indignation applicable in the case. The Spears of Phineas should end them in this world and the toasting fork of Satan in the next.

The diseases of humanity are traced by science more and more to this source. The emotions of joy are, and cannot be exaggerated, at a marriage. The profusion of wine in this case, more than could possibly be drunk, and the frequent effusion at great festivals in Latin countries when the public fountains are made to flow with wine denote the excessive emotions, the common use of wine where every school child has his flask with dinner is in evidence.

The introduction of ardent spirits, distilled liquors, has brought drinking to the danger point. When the time comes when life is wanted enough to prevent its use, when the habitual use of distilled liquors, narcotics, sedatives, including tobacco, will be prohibited, in seeing the use of which every boy and young man I see gives me the same feeling of seeing an open vein.

In my own case, increasing disability of old age, I have found the simple life, the use of nothing but alimentary food and only pure water as a beverage and as a necessity, which has made me of such a state of health that when I was in the hospital for surgical treatment one year ago, a head S.D. and M.D., meeting me in the hall one day, said as he put his hand on me, "You will pass for a man of fifty-five."

AGAIN I WILL COME BACK to my narrative if the goblins will let me. I received a letter from Ben, who was supposed to be somewhere in the south [of California gold country], but he had gone home, seeking rest and finding none, telling of changes there, marking changes in my life and environment also.

My dearest friend at home, Francis, had married my young sister. After a brief time he went to New York and on return was taken with small pox. He was isolated by the Old Roman, his father, who sternly commanded his sister and wife to leave the care of Francis to himself. Glorious old Ben went there and assisted, was with them when they died, and spoke of the affection manifested between father and son. They dug a grave in the garden, and "they buried him darkly at the dead of night and in the sheets as a shroud they wound him, the struggling moonbeam's misty light the lantern dimly burning."[38]

Bitter tears were shed on the other side of the continent. The last letter I had from Francis seemed to presage his early death, as he spoke of my coming to his grave at sunset, and so on. This priceless letter, with all others, went in the Indians' raid.

The uncertainty of gaining money and the certainty of my present life and environment from friendship and love, which I longed for as "The hart panteth for the water-brook,"[39] determined me to leave California. Jerry and I intensely cursed the Trinity and all connected and determined to leave, I for home and he for the south. He had not been as long as I in the country, so his saving had been less. We told Phillips and left all to him instead of selling. In the first part of June 1853, one morning we bade him farewell.

"Here," says he, "give me that old hat of yours. The Trinity River wants that."

I had an old straw hat I had kept sewed together as a sun shield, worn winter and summer. I had a head of hair like an Indian who never has a head covering. So he caught it from my head, twirled it three times around his head, and sailed it into the stream, an offering to the river-god or devil, I don't know which.

---

[38] From "The Burial of Sir John Moore after Corunna" by Charles Wolfe.
[39] Psalm 42:1.

IV: Heading Back

We arrived at the summit after our seven-mile rise and as we turned, I said "Jerry, we shall never see that prospect again."

"Not by a — sight," says he.

☙

WE MADE OUR THIRTY-MILE tramp in time for dinner, booked our stage ride for the next morning and rested. The next morning at six o'clock, the stage was brought round with its four splendid horses, show animals, the first on the route. We were first booked. I choose my seat on the top, back of the driver for a good lookout, with the editor of the *Shasta News* at my side. Thirty of us rode inside and out on that memorable ride, over some two hundred miles. We came to Clear Creek from the Divide, a steep descent down to the water as deep as the horses could keep their footing, down and through at full speed.

"Take hold of my collar," said the driver. I did so, not knowing what he meant. "Hold on like Hell."

"All right, I will." I braced myself.

We went down, through and up, the driver, with his long whip constantly in action on the leaders, kept things straight; dust in evidence. After some ten or twelve miles, the horses, wet and the color of the road dust, were unhitched at another station and changed for a team as clean as water could make them. A man held each at the head until hitched, then at the word, "Let go," the wild ones at the pole and the half-tame at the lead, with buckskin and profanity in unison, the wheelers, one up and another down, it was go or be dragged. After some miles of this, the horses found it easier to take their places in a line of least resistance, like other members of social life.

The passengers were of all ranks, from the editor of the paper, Jerry and I returning to civilization after four years' absence, down to the Chinese laundryman. We crossed the Sacramento at Caluso to the east side on a ferryboat big enough to drive onto without unloading. At nightfall, we stopped for a meal at an irrigated ranch, our first knowledge of what can be done by irrigation. I saw the first reaper I had ever seen in motion; a tribe of Indians were in the corral, living houses made by the direction of white men, clean, dressed in spotless white; waiters and fan-swingers; we sat down in "the kingdom of heaven" to our well-cooked and well-served repast, then up and away again.

In the night at the crossing of the Feather River, the boat grounded and it took an hour of the utmost labor and profanity to get across. Then the crack team was hitched to make the ten miles into the city of Marysville at the junction of the Feather and Yuba Rivers with the American River, where gold was first discovered.

We were behind time on account of detention at the ferry, so when we approached straight and several miles unobstructed by sight, it was Sunday morning. All Marysville looked out to see the stage come in, the driver standing up with buckskins and yells, every horse at the utmost speed. We came to the first hotel of the city in a cloud of dust, where we changed stages. The stage was ready, with horses hitched and driver in his seat.

As we brought up, he shouted, "This stage starts for Sacramento in fifteen minutes."

We hustled for the dining room. The gentlemen and ladies in their boiled clothes gave us place in a hurry. I didn't want more than five minutes to get a meal in those days, to secure my place with time to spare.

We came into Sacramento about two o'clock, too late for steamboat or stage to the southern mines. I was to take the boat and Jerry the stage. We got a meal, took a bath, and for the last time I cleaned myself of dust of California. I went to the daguerreian gallery for my picture, then to the barber shop for my hair cut and shave, and came back shaven and shorn with my picture. Jerry was disgusted and expressed himself accordingly.

"Picture? No good. No expression. Don't look like you. If I had your beard, I'd never have shaved," and so on.

I thought, "Not promising for entering civilized life," as we shook hands in reciprocal friendship; one of the best fellows I ever knew. We kept up a correspondence for a long time in after life.

IV: Heading Back

17. Leaving California

ONCE MORE ALONE. Wandering, I met a man I knew on the *Samoset*. There were two brother, Edward and Amos Faville of York State, good fellows.

"Hello, Ed Faville, the world is not very big, is it?" And we shook hands. "Where is your brother Amos?"

"He is in Australia. Here is a letter I just had from him. He said that it is a God-forsaken country. He has made more than he probably would have made here. He is going home now."

Thus momentarily meeting, we meet and part on life's sea.

I came down on the boat to San Francisco. There was a man who came later, C. S. Weston, from nearby at home. He went north with us but made a brief stay. He had written to me that he was going home on the next semi-monthly steamer, so I expected to find him on board, but did not as he had taken a tramp steamer and had gone on that to Panama. I should find him on the Isthmus.

As I came into the harbor, the changes in four years were immense. The fleet of old hulks were buried. Montgomery Street, formerly on the beach, was inland. By reason of a wrong signal, a steamer rammed into the wharf and half way through it. Ashore, looking around, I saw no familiar objects. It had been burnt over several times. Gambling hells in full blast. Not so crowded as formerly. Disguised gamblers on the outside, as returned miners winning money. Prostitutes loaded with gold and jewelry. If there is one object I detest the sight of, it is gold. I have seen it in profusion on the vilest men and women on earth. Looks to me much as human scalps. I never wore a gold watch chain. Of course, labor must be put in cold-storage some ways, and that is the most concentrated form at present available, but *ad nauseum*. I had sent home my savings before I went north. In case of contingencies, I was not encumbered with much.

A belt around me, I booked my passage home on the Steamer Golden Gate. I paid the same that I paid around Cape Horn, to sail the next day. I wandered around, went over towards the mouth of the harbor, took a parting swim in Pacific waters. I had heard of *Uncle Tom's Cabin* by Mrs. Stowe, found it in cheap form, and bought it for amusement on board.

I saw San Francisco over the stern of the vessel, receding in the distance as I had longed for so long. The ship made a call for mail at Monterey, Santa Barbara, San Diego. California, good-bye! I had graduated and left school, character formed, feared neither man nor devil, thought I could hold my own with either, still think so. Change of scene and environment, monotony of conditions of sea life.

☙

WE STOPPED AT ACAPULCO for coaling, a small land-locked harbor. We came in in a gale of wind and were immediately in a calm. Coal in bags, a procession of Mexicans of both sexes immediately in the gang-plank putting it on board. We went ashore for something to eat and to look around. Rushed to the first eating house. No meat, but chicken, broiled, served in halves; got mine scarcely warmed through; uncooked chicken is not appetizing. Paid one dollar. Left. Found a French sign further back. Went for that. Lesson: Never in traveling go to the nearest eating house. Food not good. Go to French sign. Best cooks on earth.

It's miserable country around Acapulco. It has a railroad now. We took on cattle for food. We would see a canoe coming alongside; we would see a pair of bullock horns lashed to each side. A rope from the yard arm of the ship lowered, tied to the horns: "Haul away." A skeleton covered with hide would emerge from the water, hauled some thirty feet, took by the tail, swung around over the cattle pen and lowered. We were fed on that. The vilest meat I ever ate. Not a cheek full of fat in it, and the bones pounded up. Tasted like carrion.

We got some fruit. Best pineapples I ever ate. Ripe and juicy. I was some seasick all the time at sea. I found some good fellows as usual, a party of them having lunch, a pile of claret, and so on. We were approaching Panama. I had some pineapples I could not eat.

"Here are some pineapples I shall not use. Will you like them?"

They would. "On condition that you take lunch with us."

"Well, I won't butt in."

"Nothing of the kind. Come on."

Gentlemen all. Pleasant time. Good friends. Open roadstead. Old Spanish town, like a picture, walled in ancient fashion to the open horizon. I saw many serpents about two feet long with yellow stripes. Read of them afterwards—the only sea-serpents known; poisonous.

☙

IV: Heading Back

WE LANDED AT PANAMA on the first of July about nine o'clock. I immediately proceeded to book my effects in water-proof bags for Cruces and prepared myself for walking twenty-five miles over the divide to the Chagres River. Many of the passengers had hired horses at sixteen dollars, or one doubloon. I knew I could get there sooner on foot, so with the friends I lunched with, I brought an umbrella to keep the blazing sun off and started. To guard against the cutthroats, I did not carry a pistol, as I expected to be drenched in the thunder storms, but I had a short, strong knife I knew would not misfire. We proceeded across the intervening space to the foothills. I remonstrated at the gale. My companions said it would take two days.

"Two days for twenty-five miles," said I. "I can walk twenty-five miles less setup endwise, in any one day I think. I am going to Cruces today."

It was about ten o'clock. Alone, I lit off. I soon overtook a horseman.

He said, "I think it is unsafe traveling alone. Suppose we keep company?"

I knew he could not. A horse cannot travel with a man on average. I said, "I am going to Cruces."

When under Spanish rule, Portobello on the Atlantic side and Panama on the Pacific were connected by a trail or so-called road. The Indians being enslaved more or less by the first settlers (as were those of New England, sold to the planters of the West Indies). A paved road some of the way, some vestige of this pavement was in evidence. The geological formation was the same as the Rio de Janeiro. No primary rocks. Hills, small and rounded. Erosion evidently very great. As we approached the divide, the trail was worn down some fifteen feet by the constant passing of pack and riding animals. Dense growth of tropical vegetation on sides. Each side impassible. Each animal had to keep to the track. The holes made by the tracks of three or four hundred years, the length of a horse's legs.

As we came near the summit, the daily evaporation being immense, lightning broke up the heated air strata on the surface, and made the region inhabitable, resulting in the most terrible showers on earth—something I never saw before. Thunder and lightning and rain almost solid. The track two feet deep. Liquid accumulations of the filth of centuries. Of course, the two-feet holes were unseen. It was down and up in mud indescribable. I wallowed through to Cruces, the mud for the last ten miles would average more than knee deep.

I got through at about sunset. I think the foremost. I had on a new pair of shoes when I started. They were torn to pieces and hung on my ankles. I bought a dry shirt and a pair of slippers, and went down to the river. The showers had raised it six feet, a stream usually the volume of the Housatonic River. I stripped, washed myself and my clothes, wrung them out and put on the dry shirt; I wore but two garments. I went up to the roadhouse where I stayed, sat down at a table, and called for black tea. Best drink for a tired man on earth. I drank nine cups.

Now give me some blankets. They pointed me to the loft. I laid off my wet clothes and got into blankets. Took a sweat. The next day I was all right and could take another tramp. At nine or ten o'clock, the procession began to arrive. A sorry-looking set, having stayed in open sheds, sleeping on raw hides. Horsemen were sore from bruises from the animals floundering and being pitched overhead. Soon the gold, mail, and baggage train arrived.

We put on a fleet of boats for Barbacoas, twelve miles down, where we took the railroad over twenty-five miles to Aspinwall (now Colon). At Barbacoas we took dinner where the railroad crossed the river.

The most efficient eating house was run by old Joe Prince, a Jamaica Negro who weighed some over three hundred pounds and dressed in broadcloth and stovepipe hat. The way he strutted around and damned his colored waiters was great. He gave us good things to eat: turtle and all tropical dishes and fruits. While we were at dinner, we heard the whistle of the locomotive and we broke into cheers. Then no one was to be left, as the U. S. Mail was to be forwarded, and the devil would literally take the hindmost.

The recklessness of man is indescribable. I saw one man dead drunk and his life depended on his not being left behind the mail. He got through, though. I saw him afterwards in Detroit, Michigan. Another came to me. He had a through ticket, but had not money to pay for a ticket on the railroad. Nine dollars. I didn't know whether he was a deadbeat or not, but his life depended on the ticket, I thought, so I bought and gave one to him. Said he had friends in New York and would pay me there.

We boarded the cars for Aspinwall, and got there at dark. The steamer *Illinois* was waiting for New York, another steamer for New Orleans. Tramp steamer *Columbia* and *Golden Gate* on the Pacific, so two loads on the Atlantic went to their destination. I expected to find

IV: Heading Back

Weston had come down on the tramp steamer, so I went into the waiting building where there were nearly one thousand passengers. I saw him and went and tapped him on the shoulder.

"Hello, Colonel."

We had slept under the same blanket, but he did not know me shaven and shorn.

"You don't know me," said he.

"I think you do," I shouted.

"What the____! Is this you, Buckingham?"

"I think so."

"Well, we must get aboard."

It was about two o'clock a.m. The tide was in. A plank passway some six feet wide and as steep as we could ascend was provided, no railing at the sides. We dragged our baggage in the darkness through the crowd— the water twenty or thirty feet below. There was a lantern at the upper end where each one delivered his ticket to get aboard. I had carried my ticket on my person from San Francisco. It looked like a wet paper wad.

"Here is my ticket. Handle it carefully so as I know it."

He picked a piece off and threw it into the box. "Pass on."

I thought if I had bought a ticket to Panama, then a wad of old paper would have passed on the Atlantic. Soon all were aboard. The screams of the whistle bade farewell to the Isthmus on the Fourth of July, but we did not celebrate.

18. Sailing Home

My reminiscences are of the average man in which history is ever making as in the present and the "coming events cast their shadows before,"[40] as applied to scenes of life on the Isthmus of Panama on which the world's interest is concentrated and which the man of an average ability was impressed at the time and is now.

I am impelled to review conditions and speak of the relative importance on the continents of North and South America, between two oceans, their commerce following the action of gravity. The watershed

---

[40] The title of a book by Keith Conway, 1859.

denoting the ocean on which the worldwide distribution is made, the importance of the canal in the world's commerce is shown. There is no navigable river from the Straights of Magellan to the Golden Gate. The watershed will not average more than one hundred miles from the coast.

The continent of South America, the most productive body of land on earth, is almost all on eastern slope with the greatest of navigable rivers, the products of the strip on the Pacific are almost exclusively mineral, commercially is also North America, though California and Oregon may be considered as agricultural, recently developed. These products, most of which are of perishable order, will be sent by railroad. The products of Eastern Asia and Australia are so equally balanced between East and West and the voyage stations so contiguous, that the balance will seem to me in favor of the West.

֍

WE MUST GO BACK to first principles. Philosophers say there is in the universe a power that makes for righteousness, ever advancing, casting aside what does not fit conditions, selecting what is fitted for conditions, and the discovery of those acting on comprehensible facts. Science is the sum of all human knowledge and progress. Most beings call this God. St Paul, that matchless lawyer to state a case, preached to the Athenians, as One who made the world and all therein is in whom we live and move and have our being.

It is said that the fear of God is the beginning of wisdom. It may be added that the knowledge of God is its consummation as perfect love casteth out fear. The God St Paul preached of is the God of Love. Does a man love his life, does he love as the motive of his being? The first command is that he love God with all his soul, might, mind, and strength; it is a reasonable command and comes from the nature of the relation. When man sees himself surrounded by destructive forces, not knowing the love that points the way, whatsoever a man soweth, that shall he also reap, or as Emerson says, "What will you have in the Market? Take it and pay the price,"[41] and I might add don't whine if you make a bad bargain.

We pray for deliverance from lightning and tempest, not realizing what especially in tropical regions, were it not for the automatic action

---

[41] From *Emerson on Transcendentalism*, by Ralph Waldo Emerson.

IV: Heading Back

in breaking up the air-strata and the rushing winds, life would be impossible, plague, pestilence, and famine. Comprehensible causes controlled by cleaning up malaria swamps, irrigating deserts, occupying the earth, and subduing it. Battle, murder, and premature death, organizing government and making sanitary conditions, we grope in the case darkly and are warned as the child is by putting its hand in the fire of destruction inevitable. "I have never seen an abstract sinner."

Man seeks his greatest good, as he things, and cause and effect is binding and inevitable on God and man cannot be avoided. The sin can be, the effect never. Everything is from cause. When the disciples asked Christ, "Why cannot we do such a miracle?" he said, "Such only comes through prayer and fasting." There was no interruption of cause and effect, but he was inspired by communion with a higher power, always open to any human being.

So, when we pray for deliverance from evil, the answer is as Moses at the Red Sea. "Why cryest thou unto me? Speak unto the children of Israel that they go forward."[42] You have the pillar of cloud and of fire to guide, the comprehensible facts of the universe. "And eye hath not seen, ear hath not heard; neither hath it entered in to the heart of man to conceive the state of man."[43]

"When the knowledge of God shall cover the earth as the waters cover the great deep."[44] This knowledge of the straight and narrow way denotes the course by sorrow, tears, and blood. The effect of this on the Isthmus I witnessed as the lesson on building the railroad at the city of Colon. The landing and for several miles inland are impassable malaria swamp. The railroad began inland and built towards the sea, carrying earth and making a track, making land to build upon. No place can be imagined more unsanitary. The waste of human life in building the railroad was terrible. It was said there was a corpse to every tie. Many wrecks returned on the ship with me, several died and were buried at sea. The French attempted to build a canal with the cost of thousands of lives and millions in money. Comprehensible facts were ignored.

Finally, the United States took the problem, and have proceeded by experience of what not to do, and consequently what to do. It is

---

[42] Exodus 14:15.

[43] 1 Corinthians 2:9.

[44] Isaiah 11:9.

thought it would be successful. But when it was spoken of as a one hundred million dollar enterprise, I said, "When they have spent five hundred million dollars, we shall be in better position to judge whether it is possible." There has been probably the greatest erosion there on earth. As far as I am informed, there's no finding of primary rock. All rocks are course conglomerate and very friable, and that at the dam and locks covered, to an unknown depth with the debris of erosion, so there is no junction with the shell of the earth.

When the lake eighty feet above the oceans is filled some fifty feet deep, to my mind (uneducated in engineering), I have doubts of the hydraulic pressure. One thing is not doubtful. A sea level with the slide of the sides is impracticable, and this slide must continue for ages to come with the dredges always at work. There is no supposition in my mind of an income above an investment on the canal, but perhaps in no other way could a demonstration of the possible future of the stored fertilization of the tropics be utilized for humanity, when human life is made possible. Habitations are cooled by liquid air or otherwise, and the knowledge of God through comprehensible facts is ever advancing through tears and blood.

An illustration: The scientist who discovered prussic acid was lecturing on its properties, saying that this is deadly in its effects when taken internally. "But harmless when applied externally, as you will see," said he, as he poured some into his hand and fell dead. Thus knowledge advances through martyrdom.

&

ON THE STEAMSHIP *Illinois*, a good sea-going vessel, but uncomfortable plying between New York and the Isthmus. It was probably well supplied from New York outward, but with no fresh supplies on the return, or cleaning of the ship. No choice for us but to take what we can get and, as an old Negro said, "If the debble don't get the owner of this ship, there isn't any use of having a debble." We were divided into messes, but when the messes were called, each one made a rush, so that the best of the provisions went to the ones who got there first; and the next messes, the same. I spoke to the first officer of these conditions; his reply, "Can't you take care of yourself?"

"I can. I am not whining. The weaker ones will suffer here or in hell where I am. Conditions are the same here as there; the agents likewise."

IV: Heading Back

It was the nastiest place I was ever in, with a batch of laborers from the railroad sent home. We buried several at sea near the stern of the ship, the bodies sewed in canvas on a plank weighted at the feet. The officer read the burial service. At the words, "We commit the body of our brother to the great deep," the plank was tipped and was shot into the foamy wake of the ship and disappeared in a moment. The most solemn funeral I ever saw. I have seen the burning of the body of the Indian chief, with his earthly positions to be used in the spirit land; the miner in his blankets; and in the pestilence of San Francisco, without ceremony; but the burial at sea is the most impressive.

I formed an acquaintance with a good fellow of Ohio, Robert Kennedy. In the time of the war there was a General Robert Kennedy from Ohio. It might have been him. Kennedy was a good fellow, one whom one likes to meet. We were speaking of the Isthmus. I spoke of a Michigan fellow for whom I bought a ticket on a railroad.

"What?" said he. "Did he stick you?"

"Only the price of a ticket on the railroad. Are you in, too?" says I.

"Well some, about thirty dollars, commencing from San Francisco for his return ticket."

"Well," I said. "I think he is a deadbeat. He may have friends in New York who will enable him to pay, but not probably." The Michigan fellow vanished on our arrival.

We landed in New York on July 11, about one month from San Francisco. Weston was ill with Isthmus malaria fever. I remembered the boarding house on Chatam Street and took a carriage there, to dispose of our gold and so on. There, we were immediately environed with deadbeats. We went from place to place for some time before they knew what we were about and were not cheated to any great extent.

Finally I went into an unpretentious store. "Do you want to sell an outfit of clothing at a reasonable profit?"

He said, "I have been in California."

"Where?" I said. I was satisfied that he told me the truth, so we bought the outfits, trunks, and so on, and were not very much cheated. We stayed but one extra day in New York. Weston was getting worse, and I was anxious. We came into New Milford out of stage time. I went to my brother's; I had heard he was married.

He stepped back, bowed to the stranger, "Hello!"

"Don't you know me?" I shouted.

"Thunder and lightning! Is that you, Ralph?"

"No, guess not, but I'm in his place. I have no time to talk now. I want a doctor to give my friend something so that I can get him home. I must have a team at once." He went with me to Dr. Hine, who prescribed for Weston.

"Twenty-five cents," he said.

I was about to hand him five dollars.

V: BACK HOME

19. Home in Connecticut — 1853

SHOULD ONE ATTEMPT TO resume their position four years after death, all changes naturally molded by those living, new ties formed during his absence, not a ripple caused by him in life? He returns with affections fresh and clinging to those who had made new ties. There is no effect of the imagination equal to the experience.

As I came to the ancestral home, a young lady in mourning saw me and ran into the house. It was the girl I left behind me. She was with my young widowed sister, who had married my dearest friend. They were on a visit to my mother. My sister met me and we embraced. As I stepped back, the lady stepped forward and said, "Will you give me a kiss, too?"

The impulse was to take her in my arms and give her a thousand. I put my lips to hers, seemingly as cool as she. My mother entered.

"Oh my mother, there is one glad to see me, I know as glad as I am to see her. I am your boy yet."

My brother came in; there was a cradle with a child in it, and his wife a schoolmate.

"Well, I am late to kiss the bride, but I will now."

There was no lack of welcome from all I had known, but there was that feeling that the world got along without me, and I was superfluous. My sister and hers went home. The next day she came back with an earnest request from the old Colonel to come and see him without delay. I did so, and was greeted with fatherly kindness; the motherly kindness was wanting. I saw I was not on her book.

The father and daughter would have my adventures by flood and field, so we sat into the small hours and I talked until I was hoarse. The next morning he took me to his private room and with streaming eyes talked of his son, my friend, and as the Duke of Ormone said to one who condoled with him on the death of his son, the Earl of Ossory,

"I would rather have my dead son than any living son in Christendom."[45] There was almost a hope from the manner of the young lady as though there might be a possibility, but I had said I would never remind her by word or act of the past. I was upon my honor to make no advance, so I came and went, apparently welcome.

At length I came unexpectedly. There was a company of young people present, including the supposed young gentleman. The old Roman stepped forward and introduced us. I saw at the glance the conditions. He was everything that I was not, an only son through several generations, of easy circumstances a polished gentleman. Probably had never damned a man or had the luxury of a fight. No mother would hesitate for a moment between us or perhaps a daughter either.

With the stoicism of the Indian, I shook hands and expressed my pleasure of the honor of his acquaintance. I saw the unpleasantness of the situation for the mother and daughter, and soon I took my leave. I went to the garden where my friend was buried, leaned my head on the tombstone, and the episode was closed forever, leaving scars.

❧

MY CAMP MATES USED to say, "I would like to see you in a 'biled' shirt in the company of ladies." The experience: my cousin Earl Buckingham was supposed to be engaged to the lady whom he afterwards married, and he proposed an introduction of me to her and her set. Of course "Barkis was willin'."[46] So I did my best to appear civilized, and we went. I was introduced to the charming young lady.

Earl said, "Is there anything going on tonight?"

She said, "There is to be a gathering at Mr. Smith's, music and so on."

So we went there. Miss Brinsmade's school was then in full operation with the best blood of the nation. There were some from the south. I was introduced to a Miss Mary Washington form Virginia. These girls, who came from the hands of their lady mothers and were polished by Miss Brinsmade until a fly wouldn't slip up on them, were strange beings to me. Earl was a teacher of music at home. Among them I had no subject of conversation but monosyllables. The peerless lady Miss Mary Brinsmade came to my rescue, drew me to talk of conditions

---

[45] Widely quoted. James Butler, Duke of Ormone, was a companion of Charles II in exile.

[46] From *David Copperfield* by Charles Dickens.

and experiences. My tongue was loose unconsciously and I found I was the center of interest. So I abated. I had the honor of the friendship of Miss Mary Brinsmade through her life. Years afterwards when through her marriage and mine we became members of the same church, we became more intimate. She was always the peerless ideal lady.

Earl said to me afterwards, "Those girls rather like you but they say you look at them so. You must stop it, they will not bear your eyes. They are awful, they say."

"Ask those girls, if they had been in hell for four years with their sole companions devils and then were transported to heaven with all its accompaniments, whether they would not sit up and take notice?"

The Tragedy of My Dear Friend Ben

I HAVE TOLD OF Ben's disappointment in coming home and finding no place vacant for him. He returned hopeless, seeking rest and finding none; he again went home like one returned from death. I immediately went to his mother, and almost my mother (I had boarded there some two years).

"Oh, I am so glad to see you, Ralph. I want you to take Ben and make him the same as he used to be."

"Where is he?"

"He is up in his and your room."

I went up, and found him in bed. I stripped the clothes off and essayed to pull him out as we used to skylark. He immediately entered into the spirit of the case, and we had a time like of old.

"Come put on your clothes. Let's have a tramp."

He responded, but still he was not the same old Ben.

I said, "Ben, we must get out of this. Let us clear out, go west and commence life over."

"It would do well enough for you. It is too late for me."

"Shucks, you are not much older than I. We have not much but a little to start with, and we can match ourselves with anything living. Perhaps we can find a girl who will make life worth living. I have a brother in Pennsylvania. One in Michigan. And one in Illinois. I am going to see them. Go with me."

"No, I can't. I won't."

I found recollections interfered with my projects; I could not forget. I returned soon, seeking rest but finding none. Ben had also wandered and returned. One day he came where I was assisting my brother and cousin who had a road contract. He brought a book, *Byron's Poetical Works*. Said a man in New York sent it to me. I was puzzled, I could think of none who would be likely to do so. Ben I knew almost as well as myself; he was going away and this was his parting gift. No emotion visible.

"Come Ben, go and have dinner with us."

"No, not today. I take dinner with you always when I come around." He departed.

I said to them, "Ben is going away and we shall not see him soon." I never saw him again alive.

In about two weeks his mother sent for me. She said, "Ben went away about such a time, as he is the habit of doing."

"Yes," says I, "Nothing unusual for him to do."

"I wish you would look on the top of that cupboard."

I took a chair, stepped up. "There is nothing here."

"I thought so," says she, "He kept his revolver there."

"Have you looked in his trunk?"

"No."

"You stay here."

I found that his trunk was locked, but my key would open it. I thought I might find some explanation, but found nothing except the absence of one suit of clothes. I asked his mother, "What do you know? What did he say? Tell me something."

"I don't know anything. I asked him for his knife one day. He said, 'I have lost it. I dropped it in a dark place.'"

I went home and took the mental trail. His money must be pretty much gone. No one on earth knew of it or of him, but me, his line of thought and emotion. I passed a sleepless night. The next morning I went to his brother, and said "I want you and Isaac [the brother-in-law] to go with me and find Ben."

Hays he in astonishment, "Find Ben? He may be in any part of the United States or started for South America."

"That may be," I said. "But his dead body is in that ledge of broken rock." I pointed to Mt. Tom. "Or the one farther up where the hemlocks grow, or on the top of the mountain. Or we shall see him again. Come, we will get Isaac."

"What nonsense," says he.

V: Back Home

"Perhaps so. We will see."

There were broken masses forming caverns between where we school boys played. They were surprised to see me go through and out. I came to a place some twenty feet long, dark, a dim light in the farther end. My mind's picture was that this was the place. I sprang out, and shouted, "Come here. I think there is something in here. Stand by." I went in. He was there, feet visible. "He is here."

"No, it cannot be."

"He is. There is a body." I went forward, saw the face disfigured by some animal. His brother screamed. He had not treated him kindly. "You stay here. We must take the body away before night. Touch nothing until I return with help."

About a mile away, my cousin Earl's school was on an exhibition day. I called him out with my old schoolteacher, A.N. Baldwin, and told them what I found. School was dismissed.

"I will send the Justice of Peace, and men to make a jury."

I ran through the neighborhood, sending every man I met to the schoolhouse. By the time I returned, they were ready. I led them to the mountain with a blanket to wrap the body.

"Don't you let his mother see it," said I.

My finding the body was uncanny. I must have known something of this. So I talked.

"Form a jury. I will tell my story. He was not insane any more than I am."

He was in a sitting posture when it was done, as it was low overhead. He put the pistol at the side of his head, fired, and fell backwards. The pistol fell between his arm and side.

"There are no explanations. One cent in his pocket, the last one he had."

I told the amount he had when he started for home the first time, about $1900. All arrangements were left to me by his mother and brother. She was a pious old Methodist, so I arranged for religious services. The body was carried to the meeting house, but in deference to feeling of the members, it was left in the porch. I led the pallbearers and committed it to the rest. After this was done, some comment was made as to his religious life and belief with its results. I let up on the curb of my temper.

"When the priest in the Levite passed by on the other side (these Orthodox believers), the Samaritan the outcast of Israel went to the relief of the man who fell among thieves, and when it is said, 'Inasmuch as ye have done it unto the least of these my brethren, ye have done it unto me.' I should put his arm over my shoulder. 'Come, go with me.'"

My friend Jerry saw it in print and wrote to me for particulars.

I went to see the old colonel. (Ben, it will be remembered assisted in the care and burial of Francis.) He listened with pale cheeks as I told of Ben's conditions, and mine. My mother, on my showing her the revolver which the jury told me to keep, said, "Oh Ralph, don't keep it."

"Mother, don't fear. I shall never hurry away, I shall fight it out."

ಬಿ END ಬಿ

Appendix

A. The Buckingham Family

Part 1. Genealogy. Condensed excerpt from *The Buckingham Family: Or The Descendants Of Thomas Buckingham, One Of The First Settlers Of Milford Connecticut (1872)*, Frederick William Chapman, Editor. www.archive.org/stream/buckinghamfamily00chap/buckinghamfamily00chap_djvu.txt

The Buckinghams of [Milford] have been located in their appropriate place in the regular line of descent, with the exception of a few families descended from one William Buckingham, of Pennsylvania who claim that they belong to a distinct race, but whose account of their ancestor appears so confused and unreliable as to lead us to the conclusion that they are from one of the descendants of Thomas Buckingham, of Milford, that wandered off from the family hearth as late as the third or fourth generation. ...

The name Buckingham...was derived from Bucen or Becen, or Beechen —beech trees—and ham, a village, from the number and size of beech trees. ...It has been a tradition in the family that their ancestor was a Welshman. It is so recorded of his son, Rev. Thomas Buckingham, on the Saybrook Church Records, and copied by Dr. Field in his statistics of Middlesex county, that he "was of Welch extraction." As the old records of the Saybrook church are lost, if there ever were any, and those they now have are of comparatively recent origin, they are only equivalent to the common tradition. The name is, evidently, an old English name, and we should naturally look for it somewhere in or near the county of Buckingham. ...

Thomas Buckingham, the puritan settler, and ancestor of all the American Buckinghams, was one of the company to which Eaton and Hopkins, two London merchants, and the two ministers Davenport and Prudden belonged. They arrived at ... New Haven in 1636. Thomas

Buckingham removed to Milford in the autumn of 1639. ... His name stands the fifth on the list of Free Planters. ...His house lot, containing three acres, was a little above the Second Congregational meeting house, to the right, and on the corner where the old Bryan house now stands [1849] and is still in possession of his descendants on the mother's side. ...

Thomas Buckingham was twice married. (1) To Hannah, in England, by whom he had five children. She died at Milford, June 28, 1646. (2) To Ann. Unfortunately, the family name of neither of his wives has been found. ...

Samuel Buckingham, second son of Thomas Buckingham, the Puritan settler; baptized June 13, 1641; married Dec. 14, 1663, Sarah Baldwin, daughter of Timothy Baldwin, one of the first settlers of Milford. ...

Samuel Buckingham, son of Samuel and Sarah (Baldwin) Buckingham, born Nov. 1, 1668. ...He married Sarah. ...Mr. Buckingham was a proprietor in the town of New Milford, although he never moved there. He died Oct. 29, 1708. ...

Nathaniel Buckingham, son of Samuel and Sarah (Baldwin) Buckingham, born in 1702; married Sarah Smith, May 30, 1728. He ...died in 1780. ...

Abel Buckingham, son of Nathaniel and Sarah (Smith) Buckingham, born May 22, 1746; married (1) Hannah Botsford, of New Milford, Dec. 28, 1773, and settled in the northern part of New Milford, about a mile northeast of the village of Northville. Mrs. Hannah Buckingham died Sept 22, 1801. (2) Sarah Barnum. He had six sons. He died July 27, 1827, aged 81. ...

Gilbert Buckingham, son of Abel and Hannah (Botsford) Buckingham, born July 25, 1785; was twice married: (1) To Annis Stone, Dec. 5, 1813. She died June 8, 1824. (2) To widow Anna Baldwin, May 1, 1825. She was born July 4, 1788. ...

Ralph Buckingham, son of Gilbert and Anna (Baldwin) Buckingham, born May 2, 1827; married Elvira Wheaton, eldest daughter of Sherman Wheaton, and niece of Rev. Nathanael Wheaton, D. D., late President of Trinity College, Hartford, Conn., Nov. 24, 1855. Mr. Buckingham went to California in 1849, where he spent four years.

Since his return, has been engaged in farming, and resides in Marbledale, Litchfield County, Conn.

Part 2. Colloquial Family History: Thomas Buckingham
Thomas Buckingham, son of Robert from the County of Buckingham, was born 1606 and baptized in 1607 at All Hollows London Wall Parish, London. He took passage to Boston in 1637, as one of five in a company, with two ministers and two merchants, and was considered a Pilgrim. They sailed on two ships, one of which was the *Hector*. They arrived in Boston on June 26, 1637, and set sail again on March 30, 1638, and founded New Haven April 1638. He received thirteen acres of "upland," and built a house in Milford, which still stands and is still owned by descendants. In 1639, he helped establish the church in New Haven and was one of seven "pillars of the church." In 1657, he was one of the Deputies of the General Court.

Thomas is ten generations back from descendants in the early twenty-first century, who revived the *Memories of a Forty-Niner*. They didn't place headstone monuments then; instead, there is a memorial bridge in his honor that crosses the Winnapaug River in Milford.

B. Newtown Bee Entries

Several entries from the print source for *Memories of a Forty-Niner* include handwritten notations about the date when an article appeared in the *Newtown Bee*. Each article is a chapter in the edited edition. The following list shows the correlated dates noted in the print source.

1: Starting Out
— From *Newtown Bee*, Friday, November 1, 1912

2: Brazil
— *Newtown Bee*, Friday, November 22, 1912

3: Cape Horn
— *Newtown Bee*, Friday, November 29, 1912

4: Valparaiso
— *Newtown Bee*, Friday, December 13, 1912

5: Coming to San Francisco
    — No date label

6: Up the Sacramento to the Stanislaus
    — *Newtown Bee*, Friday, December 20, 1912

7: The Mining Camp on Carson's Creek
    — *Newtown Bee*, Friday, January 17, 1913

8: Ben, Phillips, and the Working Company
    — *Newtown Bee*, Friday, January 24, 1913

9: Vigilance Committee Times
    — *Newtown Bee*, January 31, 1913

10: Traveling to the Trinity River
    — *Newtown Bee*, February 3, 1913

11: Pests
    — *Newtown Bee*, February 21, 1913

12: Placer Mining in the Trinities
    — *Newtown Bee*, February 28, 1913

13: Life in Trinity County
    — *Newtown Bee*, March 7, 1913

14: Dennis B. Mooney and the Stockton Road
    — *Newtown Bee*, Friday, March 21, 1913

15: The Disputed Claim
    — *Newtown Bee*, Friday, March 28, 1912

No date labels:
    16: Starting for Home
    17: Leaving California
    18: Panama
    19: Home in Connecticut—1853

C. Editor's Notes

This text was created from a multi-generational scanned copy of clippings from the Newtown Bee. I've applied as much wit as possible in reading the dim text, and then edited for modern grammar and punctuation. Some personal and other side notes have been omitted for readability.

The footnotes and end material, including the brief excerpt from the Buckingham Family history, are all by this editor.

Researchers who require an original print of the *Newtown Bee* articles: please inquire by writing to jugumpress@outlook.com.

Annie Pearson, Jugum Press

THE NEWTOWN BEE,

Newtown, Friday, November 1, 1912.

MEMORIES OF A "FORTY-NINE'ER."

By Ralph Buckingham, Marblodale.

I have a pleasant personal acquaintance with the Newtown Bee man as he is familiarly known among us, and as I am inclined to speak of my experiences to the point of ridiculousness (as my personal enemy in debate in Town meeting made a point on me), I didn't think as The Bee man does that it would be entertaining to write for the paper as he urges me to do. But I submit this and what follows to his discretion:

Index

Aculpulco, Mexico, 84
Addison, Joseph, cited, 12fn
Alcalde (as magistrate), 31
Ambrose, Peru, 18
American River, California, 27, 36
An Essay on Man, cited, 69fn
Araucanian Indians, Chile, 16
Argentina, 11
Arthur, Jake, 3, 5
Aspinwall (now Colon), 86, 87

Baldwin, Timothy (Milford settler), 100
Barbacoas, Panama, 86
bears, bad advice, 56-57
Belcher, Sir Edward, cited, 35
Benicia, Cape Horn, 26
bird-life, Cape Horn, 13-14
Bonner, D.D., 3, 6
Bornio, Major, Alcade in California, 72
Boswell, James, cited, 3fn
Brazil
  description, 7-10
  iron deposits, 17
bridge building, on the Trinity, 62-63
Brinsmade, Mary, 95
Buckingham, Abel, son of Nathaniel, 1, 100
Buckingham, Ann, wife of Thomas, 100
Buckingham, Anna Baldwin, wife of Gilbert, 100
Buckingham, Annis Stone, wife of Gilbert, 100
Buckingham, Ben (cousin)
  death of, 95-98
  farewell party, 74-76
  leaving for home, 47
  leaving Trinity, 63
  mining experiences, 20, 28, 34-37, 41, 49
Buckingham, Earl (cousin), 94-95
Buckingham, Gilbert, son of Abel, 1, 100
Buckingham, Hannah Botsford, wife of Abel, 100
Buckingham, Hannah, wife of Thomas, 100
Buckingham, Nathaniel, son of Samuel, 1, 100

Buckingham, Ralph,
  photo, 82
  son of Gilbert and Anna, 1, 100-102
Buckingham, Samuel, son of Samuel, 100
Buckingham, Samuel, son of Thomas, 100
Buckingham, Sarah Baldwin, wife of Samuel, 100
Buckingham, Sarah Barnum, wife of Abel, 100
Buckingham, Sarah Smith, wife of Nathaniel, 100
Buckingham, Thomas (of Milford), 99, 101
Buckingham, William A. (of Pennsylvania), 1, 99
The Buckingham Family: Or The Descendants Of Thomas Buckingham, cited 1, 99-101
Bulwer, Lytton, cited, 71
Byron's Poetical Works, cited, 96

Calaveras River, 27, 28, 29, 67
Caluso ferry, 81
Campbell, Thomas, cited, 76fn
Cape Frio, 7
Cape Horn, 10-14, 17
Cape pigeon, 13-14, 26
Cape Verde Islands, 4
Carson, Jim (Kit Carson's brother), 29
Carson's Creek, California, 28
"Cato," cited, 12
Chagres River, Panama, 85
Chapman, Frederick William, cited, 1, 99
Chatam Street, New York boarding house, 91
Clear Creek, on Shasta Divide, 81
Coit, Dr., 22
Coleridge. Samuel Taylor, cited, 18fn
Colon (formerly Aspinwall), 86, 89
Columbia, tramp steamer, 87
Coluso, California, 52
"Coming Events Cast Their Shadows Before," cited, 87-88
Conway, Keith, 87-88
Cosumnes River, 27, 50
cradle rocker, 58
Crossing the Line, 6

Index

Cruces, Panama, 85-86

Daggett, miner of Maine, 32-34, 35-36, 55
daguerreian gallery, 82
Dana, Richard Henry, cited, 2
David Copperfield, 94
Denver, General Games William, 51
Devereaux, Lytton-Bulwer character, 71
Dickens, Charles, cited, 77, 94
Doré, Gustave, cited, 17
Duke of Ormone, quotation, 94
Dutchess County, New York, 19

Emerson on Transcendentalism, cited, 89
Emerson, Ralph Waldo, cited, 89
enteric disease, 19-
"Exile of Erin," cited, 76

Faville, Edward and Amos, of New York, 83
Feather River, 27, 82
ferry, Trinity River, 61-63
fleas, 52-53
flooding, Sacramento River, 66
Fourth of July
    Panama, 87
    Valparaiso, 14
Free Planters, in Connecticut, 100
French Creek, California, 74-76, 78

gill netting, 60-61
gold
    geologic indications, 29-30
    in Australia, 30
    regional geography, 27
Gold Bluffs, California, 47
Golden Gate, steamer to Panama, 83, 87
grouse, 64
Gulf Stream, 3, 14

Hall, Captain James Dennis, 2, 3, 5, 35
Hamilton, Bob and Joe (brothers), 42
Hine, Colonel, 52
Hollis, Captain, 4, 10, 25
hornets, 53
Housatonic River, Connecticut, 86
house building, in the Trinities, 59-60
Howard, miner from Massachusetts, 33
Hunt, Merritt, New Milford resident, 72
Hyde, English army officer, 35

Illinois, steamer to Panama, 87, 90-91
immigrants, observations, 40
Indians
    aiding pioneers, 69
    Klamath River, 49
    Sacramento River, 48
    San Joaquin, 48
    Stockton River, 67
    Trinity experiences, 57, 60, 64, 66
Isthmus of Panama, 85-86, 89-90

Jerrold, Blanchard, cited, 17
justice, community-administered, 72-73

Kennedy, Robert, of Ohio, 91
Kings' River, California 27
Klamath River, California 47

The Lady of the Lake, cited, 49
Life of Samuel Johnson, cited, 3
Litchfield County, Connecticut, 19, 101
Living Age, magazine, 55
"Long Tom" sluicing, 58-59
Lord Hood (mountain), 7
lost love, 70
Luddington, Egbert, of Connecticut, 19

Macaulay, Thomas, cited, 17*fn*
Marbledale, Connecticut, 101
Mariposa River, California, 27
Marmion, cited, 78
Marryatt, Captain Frederick, 6
Marysville, California, 82
Mercedes River, California 27
Merwin, France, 74-75
Middlesex County, Connecticut, 99
A Midsummer Night's Dream, cited, 74
Milford, Connecticut, 1, 99
Minot, steamer, 2
Miss Brinsmade's school, 94-95
Mokelumne River (also Moquelemne), 27, 44, 50
Monte Diavolo (Devil's Mountain), California, 26
Monterey, California, 84
Montgomery Street, San Francisco, 26, 83
Mooney, Dennis B.,
    ferry proprietor, 57, 61-63, 68-70
    Stockton Road, 67

Moquelemne River (now Mokelumne), 27, 44, 50
Morehouse (miner), 30
mosquitoes, 53
Mount Aconcagua, Chile, 15-16
Mount Shasta, California, 27, 57
Murray, miner, 36

New Milford, Connecticut, 1, 49, 74, 92, 100
New Milford Rifles, Connecticut, 74
New York, return to, 91-92
Newtown Bee, cited, 1, 101-102

O'Higgins, Bernardo, 16
Old Sledge, card game, 32
Osborn, Archibald, 33

Panama, 18, 85
panning, methods, 58
Patagonia, 11, 16
pests, 52-53
Phillips, mining partner, 34, 37-39, 40, 43, 47, 50, 59, 63, 66, 80-81
The Pickwick Papers, cited, 77
Pierce, miner from New Hampshire, 47, 59, 63
Pinto, General Francis E., 27-28
pioneers, 40, 65-66, 69
placer mining
  description, 30-31
  in the Trinities, 57-63
  methods, 58-59
politics, Trinity area, 61-62
Pope, Alexander, cited, 69*fn*
Portobello, Panama, 85
porpoises, 14
Portsmouth Square, San Francisco, 19
Punta Arenas, Chile, 16

Quincy House, Boston, 78

rattlesnakes, 54-55
Reed, store owner, 34
reptiles, 54-55
Rich, Jeremiah, 78
Richards, J.A. (Jerry, mining partner), 47, 51, 59, 60, 80, 81, 98
Richards, James, 20

"The Rime of the Ancient Mariner," cited 18
Rio de Janeiro, 6, 7-10
Roaring Forties, 10

Sacramento steam boat, 82
Sacramento City, 2, 51
Sacramento River, 2, 26, 66, 81
salmon fishing, 60-61
Samoset, 2-3, 6, 7, 20, 83
San Antonio castle, Brazil, 7
San Diego, California, 84
San Francisco
  arrival, 18-19
  description, 19-25
  Montgomery Street, 26, 83
San Joaquin River, California 2, 26-27
Santa Barbara, California, 84
sawing, in the Trinities, 59
Saybrook Church Records, Connecticut, 99
Scott, Walter Scott
  influence, 37
  Marmion, 78
  The Lady of the Lake, 49, 50, 67
Scott's River, California, 65
sea life, 14, 18
seasickness, 3-4
Second Congregational meeting house, Milford, 100
Sfgenealogy, cited 2*fn*
Shakespeare, miner (nickname), 42
Shakespeare, William, cited, 42, 74
Shasta, 27, 57
Shasta News, editor, 81
Sierra Nevada, California, 27, 29
Six Mile Creek, California, 35
slickens, damaging agricultural land, 63
sluicing, 58-59, 63
small pox, 80
Smith, James M.B. (lawyer), 31, 35
Smith, Mr., of San Francisco, 20
Spanish language, observations, 15
Springfield Armory, Connecticut, 33
St Felix, Peru, 18
stage coach, Shasta to Sacramento, 81-82
Stanislaus River, California 27, 29, 34, 35
Staten Island, Tierra del Fuego, 13
Stockton City, California, 26, 27
Stockton, Commodore Robert, 36

Index

Stockton River, California, 27
Stockton Road, 50, 67
Stowe, Harriet Beecher, cited, 83
Straits of Magellan, 16
Sugar Loaf (mountain), Brazil, 7
Suisun Bay, California, 26
Sutter, Captain, 48

Table Mountain, California, 29
The Tempest, cited, 42
Tierra del Fuego, 13, 16
Trinity Alps, placer mining, 57-63
Trinity County
    Indian experience, 64-65
    tax collector, 64
Trinity Mountain, California 57
Trinity River, 46-57, 80
Tripp, miner and whaleman, 32-34
Tulare Plains, California, 26-27
Tulles, description, 27
Tuolumne River, California 27, 29
Turner, Dr., 19-23
Two Years Before the Mast, cited, 2

U.S. Mail, at Panama, 89-90
Uncle Tom's Cabin, cited, 83

Valparaiso, description, 14-17
vermin, 52-53

Washington, Mary, of Virginia, 94
waterwheel, building, 60
Watson, W., of Connecticut, 20, 25
Weaverville, California, 61, 66
Weston, C.S., of Connecticut, 83, 87, 91-92
whales, in Gulf Stream, 14
Wheaton, Elvira, wife of Ralph Buckingham, 100
Wheaton, Nathanael, President of Trinity College, 100
Whitmore, Captain, 52-53, 71, 74-76
Whitton, Sam, 33
Wolfe, Charles, cited, 80
Woodin, Mary, of Connecticut, 19*fn*
Woodin, Philo S., of Connecticut, 19

Yuba River, California, 27

www.ingramcontent.com/pod-product-compliance
Lightning Source LLC
LaVergne TN
LVHW011210080426
835508LV00007B/712